# How to plan the perfect party for your child

# How to plan the perfect party for your child

## Celebrations for all ages from one to 21

**Beverly Davies**

Editor Roni Jay

Viva Books

New Delhi | Mumbai | Chennai | Kolkata
Bangalore | Hyderabad | Kochi | Guwahati

**First Indian Edition 2010**

**VIVA BOOKS PRIVATE LIMITED**

- 4737/23 Ansari Road, Daryaganj, New Delhi 110 002
  E-mail: vivadelhi@vivagroupindia.net, Tel. 42242200
- 76, Service Industries, Shirvane, Sector 1, Nerul, Navi Mumbai 400 706
  E-mail: vivamumbai@vivagroupindia.net, Tel. 27721273, 27721274
- Jamals Fazal Chambers, 26 Greams Road, Chennai 600 006
  E-mail: vivachennai@vivagroupindia.net, Tel. 28290304, 28294241
- B-103, Jindal Towers, 21/1A/3 Darga Road, Kolkata 700 017
  E-mail: vivakolkata@vivagroupindia.net, Tel. 22836381, 22816713
- 7, Sovereign Park Apartments, 56-58, K. R. Road, Basavanagudi, Bangalore 560 004
  E-mail: vivabangalore@vivagroupindia.net, Tel. 26607409, 26607410
- 101-102 Mughal Marc Apartments, 3-4-637 to 641, Narayanguda, Hyderabad 500 029
  E-mail: vivahyderabad@vivagroupindia.net, Tel. 27564481, 27564482
- Beevi Towers, First Floor, SRM Road, Kaloor, Kochi 682 018, Kerala
  E-mail: vivakochi@vivagroupindia.net, Tel: 0484-2403055, 2403056
- 232, GNB Road, Beside UCO Bank, Silpukhuri, Guwahati 781 003
  E-mail: vivaguwahati@vivagroupindia.net, Tel: 0361-2666386

*www.vivagroupindia.com*

*Published by arrangement with*

Crimson Publishing,
a division of Crimson Business Ltd
Westminster House, Kew Road
Richmond, Surrey TW9 2ND



ISBN : 978-81-309-1489-3

Published by Vinod Vasishtha for Viva Books Private Limited, 4737/23, Ansari Road, Daryaganj, New Delhi - 110 002.

Printed and bound by Raj Press, R-3, Inderpuri, New Delhi - 110 012.

Thanks to Sarah for the bright idea and to all the party mums and party people of all ages for their contributions, especially, of course, Prudy, Henry and Neil

# Contents

# Introduction

## Why are you having a party anyway?

It is important not to lose sight of this. You are having a party because it is a special day for someone you love and you want them to be happy and have a lovely time. That is not going to happen if you get into a complete state about the organisation/expense/hassle involved.

A child's birthday party is the most important social event in their calendar, eagerly anticipated from one year's end to the next. With so much emotion riding on the occasion it can be hard to stop it ending in tears and the sad fact is that many parents spend the day guiltily longing for it to be over. This book is here to help, with lots of tension-busting ideas for good times, hints on what we know works and, just as crucially, what we found out the hard way didn't work, tips on how to spend, or save your money when it comes to the big day.

We have talked to lots of party givers, party goers and professionals to get the inside track on the current state of the party, and their comments on favourite and un-favourite parties are slotted through the book. From all this research we are forced to conclude that there is a lot of madness around these days, with parents reportedly shelling out thousands on children's birthday parties, but the fact is that what makes a party successful has very little to do with the budget and very much to do with the thought and care lavished on it.

A recent survey revealed that the average UK family spends £450 each year on children's birthdays, with as many as a quarter of parents saying that they were spurred on by the fact that they had had disappointing parties when they were children. Other research shows that while ten per cent of parents questioned admitted that their aim in throwing a birthday party was to impress other parents, nearly two-thirds actually feel anxious about what other people will think about their child's birthday party. Don't. Just try to enjoy it. It will be over tomorrow.

## A word about the organisation of the book

There are no hard and fast rules for what your child will want to do at what age, so where we have suggested parties in a particular age chapter that doesn't mean that they won't be just as suitable for others.

We start at the beginning, with an overview of what you can expect for first, second and third birthdays. These are relatively simple affairs, the catering is straightforward, and a few games may be all you need.

As things start to get more complicated, we devote a chapter each to the very important subjects of party planning, party games and party food. These apply to all age groups, but have particular significance for fourth, fifth and sixth birthday parties, where you will often invite the whole nursery or primary school class. This leads on to a discussion on party entertainers and lots of hints about how to make sure things go well when you choose one.

The Great Party Bag Debate gets its own chapter. Find out what other parents and children think about this contentious issue and discover how to keep the costs down or find an acceptable alternative.

Seventh, eighth and ninth birthdays are when your child may well opt for an expedition, a barbecue, theme park, activity or sleepover. We have all the hints to help you through, as well as a useful chapter on party politics, which may help you to avoid some of the pitfalls.

By the time they are ten lots of them will love a disco – but of course some won't, and we have some great ideas for those awkward in-between years.

Teenage parties raise all kinds of issues, of which the main concern for parents is alcohol. We have a chapter devoted to drink facts, which is full of useful information and lots of suggestions for alternatives to the standard teenage party, as well as survival tactics if there really is no choice.

When you finally reach the 21st party after all those years of party giving for your children, and whether you go for a big, formal affair or something completely different, you will deserve a moment of quiet celebration of your own. Happy days.

## Part 1

# Ages one to 10

1

# One, two, three – the fun starts here

## First birthday: baby talk

The first birthday is a real milestone so whether you have a tea party for your new mum friends and their babies, champagne and cake for the family or a weekend lunch party for fellow parents, make sure it is just what *you* want – it may be your last chance to choose for quite some time.

Hardly any of the young guests will be doing much at this stage, and they certainly won't be eating a lot, but, paradoxically, this is probably the children's party with the most catering possibilities – for the grown-ups at least. As far as the babies are concerned, there isn't going to be a huge amount of interaction but you want to mark this momentous occasion.

- Serve cold drinks for the adults, to avoid the dangers of scalding tea near crawling babies, but don't leave a glass of champagne where an inquisitive toddler could try it.
- Have food that won't hurt a baby who gets hold of some.
- If you are serving food for the babies, base it on the sort of thing your own child actually eats.
- Make sure that the other mums know what food there is so that little ones can't get their hands on anything that they are allergic to or unused to eating.

★ Don't forget to capture this unrepeatable occasion on camera.

> "For my son's first birthday we had someone with a guitar singing all the babies' favourite songs like The Wheels on the Bus and Little Bo Peep. The older babies sat on their mums' knees and joined in. Everyone really loved it. The little ones still seem to know all the traditional songs these days, the bigger ones can do the actions that go with them, and all the mums know them too. We had about ten children, each with a parent. It was a hot day so we had a paddling pool in the garden, some of our guests could walk, some could still only crawl, but they all enjoyed that. For the cake I made a number one in sponge and covered it in a thin layer of icing decorated with Smarties." CLAIRE, MOTHER OF TWO

## Second birthday: treats for tea

Two and three year olds will be so delighted by the idea of having a few friends round to play for an hour or so, with a special birthday tea, that you can keep things pretty simple for this age group. Two year olds are too young to appreciate many organised games, but there are a few old favourites that they love, such as pass the parcel, and they all enjoy dancing and balloons, so you could have some simple musical joining-in games and toys for them to play with. Singing 'Happy Birthday' and lighting all two candles is the high point of the party, and they will find a fancy cake very exciting indeed. At going-home time they will be very happy with a balloon and will almost certainly let go of the string within a couple of minutes of leaving the party. Chase as you will, you probably won't catch it, giving them an early opportunity to benefit from a lesson in the inevitability of loss.

If you are inviting more two year olds than adults, the safest thing will be to serve their tea picnic-style with rugs and cushions on the floor – it is a lot less far to fall. You can make life easier by giving everyone a little pre-assembled food-box with a drink carton and food inside.

## Party food that they will actually eat

- ★ This age group is pretty easy to cater for. They love small things – little sausages, cherry tomatoes, slices of cucumber, carrot sticks, cubes of cheese, tiny sandwiches and the occasional Hula Hoop are always popular.
- ★ Make the sandwiches more interesting by cutting them into tiny triangles or little shapes made with food cutters. Or make sandwiches using one side brown bread and one side white. Cut them into little squares and arrange in a chessboard effect – a very good way of introducing some healthy brown bread into the equation.
- ★ Cut a cheese and tomato pizza into little sections that children can easily manage to eat with their fingers – one pizza will go a long way if the pieces are small enough.
- ★ Apple juice probably stains the least when spilled – as it almost certainly will be.
- ★ If you care at all about your soft furnishings you might want to avoid anything very chocolatey.
- ★ Some varieties of vanilla ice cream stain party clothes almost indelibly. If you decide to have ice cream choose a brand that you know washes out.

## Play time

At this age they will enjoy playing with the birthday child's new toys and probably won't have the concentration for too many organised games, but, with a bit of adult help, pass the parcel never fails, especially if you attach a sweet or a little present to each layer and make sure that the music stops at each child so that, miraculously, everybody wins something.

A little group of two year olds may well enjoy getting in a circle with some musical instruments like bells and tambourines and singing a few familiar songs. That can help any shy ones to join in a bit, especially if you get them to hand out the instruments at the beginning. If none of the mums or dads is particularly musical it may be a real help to have a CD of the children's favourite songs handy.

The party child can be a little overwhelmed by the presence of lots of children in the house, playing with the new toys and bringing presents that are not to be opened until later. If it all goes wrong, and it may, there is nothing much you can do apart from giving your overwrought child a bit of space and special attention to help them calm down so that they can enjoy at least some of the party. This kind of meltdown, which will probably need your undivided attention, is one of the reasons why you should enlist a reasonable amount of help from other adults at even a small party.

> "We had a teddy bears' picnic for my daughter and a friend when they were both two. We were a group of ten: four children and mums, and two baby siblings .We went to a park that is quite near home for an hour or so in the afternoon, after everyone had had their nap. We often go there, but the children knew that this day was special because they each had to bring their favourite teddy with them. We all sat in a circle on picnic rugs for tea. The menu was honey sandwiches, little sausages and tomatoes, teddy-shaped biscuits and cartons of apple juice and the cake was three bears in a bed. Apart from tea we just had a little pass the parcel game, a bit of running around and then we played hunt the teddy,

where the mothers and the children had to search for little teddies, one for each child, that we had 'hidden' in very obvious places around our picnic. The teddies were the going home presents, so we played that last."

CASSIE, MOTHER OF ONE

## Third birthday: full of bounce

Three year olds are just beginning to be a tiny bit independent, but a lot of them will still want their mum or dad to stay. They love musical games and running around. Channel all that energy with something organised like trampolining and some simple games.

### Party giving advice from nannies

Because nannies take a professional interest in children's parties and are involved in giving a number of them over time, they are an excellent source of the kind of calm and considered expertise that you can use to make your own children's party run more smoothly.

- You need the confidence to know that you can keep things going, and to some extent that confidence comes from getting really organised in advance. When you have lots of two and three year olds dropped off at different times there is a lot of milling around to start with, so you need an activity that they can start on as they arrive. This could be something like making a party hat with materials you have already laid out, so that they are all grouped round a table until everyone has arrived, or playing with some toys you have put out for them. Try to keep everyone together at this stage.

★ Parties tend to be a bit too long for younger children. People think there is a rule that they have to be for two hours, whereas in fact you will often get a happier result with a party that goes on for an hour and a half. Otherwise some of the children may start getting a bit restless, and that is when the bad behaviour kicks in.

★ Two hours is a long time to fill. You always think the tea will last for ages, but actually it doesn't because they are all excited and you get to the cake much sooner than you think, at which point you may be left wondering what on earth you can do next.

★ Write a plan beforehand and put in far more than you think you will need. Things will always go much more quickly than you expect when you actually have the children there, and you have to allow for the fact that they may not be as interested in doing some things as you expect them to be, so you need options so that you can move on quickly.

★ If you were doing songs for little ones then you might think that you could allow 20 minutes for ten songs, but you should always have another five on your list. Then, if it is going well you can go on for longer, if it is not going brilliantly you can move rapidly to something else. The important thing is to keep the party going along smoothly and not have to stop and think about what to do next. You are trying to make sure that they all enjoy themselves.

★ Pass the parcel with a forfeit appropriate to their age and a little wrapped thing on every layer is a huge success with lots of age groups, and forfeits make the game last for quite a lot longer. When they are three you can have stuff like counting to ten or hopping in a circle on one leg as your forfeits and the game can last for a nice long time. You have to make sure that everyone gets a go because it can be rotten for a little child to feel left out.

## Helping shy children

Some little children are completely fazed by a big group and don't know how to join in. The best thing to do then is to get them to help you do something like put balloons up or carry something around. Keep them with you for a while and try to make them laugh a bit and then slowly introduce them into a game.

> "A good ice-breaker for little children aged two or three is a game where you have picture cards showing different animals – sheep, ducks, cows, dogs, cats – all the ones that make sounds that they know. Each child is given a card, there are two for each animal, and they have to go round making the noise of that animal until they find the other one the same, who is then their partner until the end of the game, when everyone is in twos. When they are too young to find a pair they could still make the animal noises." RACHAEL, MOTHER OF TWO

## Calming down tips

When they are really little – one and two – it is fine to let them run around a bit, playing in the garden and so on, as long as there are plenty of toys to go round and no argument about who plays with what. By the time they are three they probably need a bit more entertainment and structure and you need a lot of adult help if they are doing anything active. You can't really just have them all dropped off and left for the afternoon – it is too much responsibility for one adult.

★ You need some help if you are having more than just a few children, but you need to ask friends who you know will join in.

★ The liveliness of this age group can be a bit hard to control, especially when little boys get really hyped up and they start running around, but you have to keep them in check or the whole thing can easily get a little out of hand.

★ You can suddenly go "Put your hands on your head" or something else a bit silly and get them to copy you if you need to calm them down instantly.

★ Sleeping lions is a great game for them. They have to lie down and see who can keep the stillest. Keep this going for as long as possible and they will start to calm down.

## Checklist

★ It's best not to invite too many children. Between five and ten is plenty at this age.

★ Two hours is the maximum sensible duration; make sure you put this clearly on the invitation, and make sure that the grown-ups don't get too comfortably settled in – it isn't their party, and over-tired children waiting for Mummy to finish her chat and her glass of wine are not going to contribute to the fun of the proceedings.

★ If anyone is going to get over-excited and behave horribly it is almost certain to be the birthday child. Expect the worst.

★ With all under-fives it is probably worth skimping on chocolate as much as possible, on behavioural as well as mess-avoidance grounds. But it *is* a party, and however much you disapprove of sweet stuff they will probably want some. If you make the birthday cake a chocolate one, that should be quite enough.

"At our daughter's third birthday party she and her friends had a lovely time bouncing around for ages on our old sofa. It was never the same after that, so when our son was three we got him a little trampoline for his birthday and had a heavily supervised trampoline session in the garden as a high point of the party fun. That age group really loves to bounce!" BENITA, MOTHER OF TWO

"For my son's third birthday I made up an assault course in the garden. We had a potato and spoon race, and a slide, and the paddling pool with some balls in, instead of water, so they had to go through that on the course. Then I put things in the sand pit that they had to find and pick up – little things for them to keep, like bouncy balls. I gave each of them a cup with their name on it, so any prizes they won they could put in the cup to take home at the end." CLAIRE, MOTHER OF TWO

## Eco-friendly parties – start as you mean to go on

While never wishing to lose sight of the fact that parties are meant to be fun, they can be intrinsically wasteful in all kinds of ways. However, there is a lot you can do to cut down on waste, and it is never too soon to start.

★ If you are looking for something worthwhile to put in the party bags, or an activity for the party, go to **www.petitartisan.com** to find craft kits, party bags and party kits for children based on natural recyclable safe materials – all things that can be made in one session, so ideal for craft parties or going home bags.

★ At **www.sillyjokes.co.uk** you can get compostable cups and plates and even wooden cutlery.

★ Steer clear of worries about latex allergies and waste with colourful Japanese paper balloons from **www.okinami.com**.

★ Get the whole party bag done for you at **www.ethicalparty bags.com** which sells green gifts for children. Fair trade chocolates, toys and footballs, alongside bracelets, pens and pads made from recycled materials are packed in nice-looking pink bags made from old juice cartons that girls will use again, or recycled brown bags for boys. The children are delighted with their going-home gift and your conscience is clear.

★ You will find only hand made, fair trade, recycled and eco friendly things at **www.earthmotherpartybags.com** including party tableware made of 100% recycled plastic, recycled paper party bags, and fair trade fillers including felt flower hairclips, recycled iPod bags, bamboo whistles and balloon boats (**07913 849791**).

2

# Planning your party

Having parties at home rather than at dedicated party venues can save you quite a bit of money. A recent survey of 500 families found that the 'at home' brigade saved up to 50% – and that can really mount up over a few children and a few years. On the other hand, sometimes it is worth every penny to hand the whole caboodle over to someone else. A lot of the same basic planning applies equally whether you are at home or away:

★ When you are picking a date for the party check in your diary to make sure it doesn't clash with any of the moveable feasts like Mother's Day or Easter Sunday. Double-check dates with other parents in the class, just in case you get two parties planned for the same day.

★ For summer holiday birthdays do check in advance whether enough children will be around to celebrate, and if not, think about moving the party to the end of the summer term or start of September, and have a small celebration on the actual day.

★ Start planning the party at least four or five weeks in advance so you have plenty of time to get all the bits and pieces you need, especially if you are ordering online.

★ If you are having helium balloons, get them delivered. A lot of party businesses do this now and it does make life a lot easier.

- ★ Break the party time down into sections in your plan so you have a good idea of what is going to happen when.
- ★ Plan to have the meal around half-way through. If you have it sooner the children may not be hungry yet and might run off to play too soon; any later and the slower eaters might not get to do any more activities before home time. You definitely want quite a bit less time to fill after tea than before.

## Invitations

- ★ Send the invitations out about four weeks before the party and make them very specific about start and finish time. Include clear information on the date and which birthday it is, your address and phone number and the date you need the reply by.
- ★ If the children need to wear special clothing – outdoor stuff/swimming gear/clothes they can get messy in/fancy dress – do say so clearly.
- ★ You may need to include a map of how to get to your house or the party venue.
- ★ If you don't know everyone who is coming put in a request for parents to let you know if their child has any special dietary requirements or allergies.
- ★ If your child is at school or nursery and isn't inviting the whole class then it is best to post the invitations to avoid hurt feelings.

- ★ Check with your child the names of the guests to be invited, including surnames if possible, or you may end up with the wrong child.
- ★ Get the birthday child to help with the invitations. They like to feel involved, and if they are keen on art they can decorate the invitations, too.

## Planning a party at a venue

- ★ Visit the venue well in advance to make sure it is what you want, and book in good time, making sure you get the contact name of someone who can help you with any future queries.
- ★ Check what you need to provide and what is there already (vital if you are bringing the food to know what there is in the way of serving utensils, kettle and other equipment). For instance, do you need to bring your own tablecloths, plates, cups, cutlery and serving trays?
- ★ Work out how many helpers you will need to bring and find out whether the venue provides anyone to help arrange furniture and carry things around.
- ★ Ask whether you can decorate the venue as you want, and if you will be able to get in beforehand to do so.
- ★ Check there are power points where you, or the entertainer, might need them.
- ★ Work out how you are going to transport everything to the venue. If your carload is going to include all the food and drink, party games, prizes, balloons, filled party bags and decorations, as well as some children, then you will probably need to enlist some extra help from a friend with a car.

- Remember mopping up cloths and bin bags, camera, portable CD player, with your own compilation of your child's favourite music or one of the children's compilation CDs and some spare batteries.
- It is *vital* to remember candles for the cake, matches and a cake knife.
- Take a big bag to keep all the presents safely together to take home later.

## Planning a party at home

- Check each room you will be using with a fresh eye for hazards – wires that could be tripped over, stuff that could get knocked down by a fast-moving posse of four year olds. Your children are used to negotiating your house, but the party guests won't be.
- Remove any low-lying ornaments to a place of greater safety and try to have one room that is not part of the party where you can put things that could be in the way.
- Put a big, clear label on the loo door.
- Don't worry too much about making the house immaculate before the party. None of the guests will notice, and you will probably have to have a bit of a clean up afterwards anyway.
- Ideally, if you can, have separate rooms for eating and playing, and have somewhere safe where you can put the presents until afterwards.

## Picking a theme

- ★ Whether it is for the whole party, such as a pirate party or a fairy party, or just for the decorations, such as your child's favourite colour, a theme makes deciding what you need to buy for the party much easier.
- ★ If there is something that your child is currently obsessed with – whether outer space, magic, some old superhero or another, Barbie or pirates, it might be fun to base the party around it. Do check that they are still keen on whatever it is before you go too far with your plans – young tastes can change rapidly, and there is no going back once they have gone off something.
- ★ Pop stars, wild animals, pirates, aliens and magic (especially Harry Potter) themes are all popular.

### Pyjama party

Children can bring their teddy bears to this sleepover. Start this party quite late, have supper and a DVD and then get ready for bed, drink cocoa, have a midnight feast, play spooky charades or tell ghost stories until it is time to go to sleep – far too late. (Parents, brace yourselves for a bumpy start the next morning.)

### Pirate party

When the children first arrive, get them to decorate pirate hats with some black card that you have cut out into shape. Have lots of stickers and things like feathers to decorate them with and crayons to draw skull and crossbones on them. That way they all have something to do the minute they walk in and they can take home their party hat at the end. Play things like musical islands and hunt for buried treasure. Then put any leftover pirate accessories away in a safe place because you may well be using them again in a few years (see Chapter 14 on parties for 18 and 21 year olds)

"A pirate party is really easy to theme. For my son's birthday I adapted lots of games, like pin the nose on Captain Pugwash, and I was particularly pleased with one idea. Instead of doing all the layers for pass the parcel I adapted it to the wonderfully labour-saving game of musical hat. We just passed a pirate hat around the circle and whoever had it when the music stopped got a sweet and did a pirate-type forfeit (doing a jig, singing a sea shanty, pretending to eat a rat) and the big prize came at the end of the game when everyone had had a turn. You can use this game for lots of different parties, it is just as good as pass the parcel, but you don't have all the wrapping up to do or all the paper to clear away at the end."
RACHAEL, MOTHER OF TWO

"When my son was four we gave him a pirate party at home. His brilliant nanny organised most of it, as I had just had another baby, and it was his best party ever. The children wore fancy dress, everyone was given eye patches to wear as they arrived, I made a pirate ship cake, and there were lots of lovely games. A treasure hunt, with easy clues leading to a blood-curdlingly ghoulish prize, pin the beard on the pirate, and lots more, all tailored to that age group. At the end we had a hunt all over the house for pirate loot, which was actually lots and lots of 1p and 2p coins. Everyone had a little swag bag and there were trails of coins all over the house. At that age, finding your own money is very exciting, and you don't really know what it is worth. So that solved the party bag issue, too. They all just took their loot home." JANE, MOTHER OF THREE

## Magic party

Thanks to Harry Potter, witches and wizards are all the rage. You could have a magic wizard dressing up party, where guests can make wands, learn some simple magic tricks and have some little tricks to take home in the party bags. Serve magic potion drinks from a cauldron (aka a large casserole dish if you don't have the real thing to hand) and you could even have a real magician to entertain them.

## Halloween

This is the best party of the year for dressing up, and costumes can be really easy to put together.

★ A simple black cloak, as worn by witches, wizards and some devils since time immemorial, will take you almost anywhere. Get a piece of black material (length according to height of child) and turn the top over about three inches and sew along. Sew again about one inch up from the first line of sewing. Thread black ribbon through this one-inch seam and you will have a cape with a frilled collar. Note: in different colours for different parties this simple piece of sewing will take them just about anywhere as kings and queens, fairies, knights, and even the odd superhero.

There are masses of great traditional games that everyone loves, such as bobbing for apples, and murder in the dark, and some variations such as pass the rat. All you need for this is a plastic rat (or spider, or anything else gruesome) which will last from year to year, and a selection of ghoulish forfeits for the person left holding the rat when the music stops.

You can let your imagination run riot with gruesome food, which only leaves the vexed question of trick or treating, and how to do it safely, without annoying the neighbours. Many parents have, at best, mixed feelings about this practice, but children do not generally share their reservations. Little children have to be supervised if trick or treating, middle-sized ones should be discreetly supervised, perhaps by an older sibling or babysitter if a parent is too embarrassing. You can forewarn a few kind neighbours that they may expect a ghoulish visit, and even give them some sweets to offer back to the trick or treaters. Try to make sure that your children don't go anywhere they will not be welcome. Some elderly people living alone might well find the whole thing offensive, or even upsetting.

> "My ninth birthday party was Halloween themed. My mum dressed up as Dracula and switched off the lights when we were telling ghost stories so some girls actually started crying. It was my best party of all time. The food was eyeball jelly and fingers with blood (chips with ketchup) and we played some great games. One was where we sat in a circle with the lights off and passed creepy things around (peeled grapes = eyeballs, cold spaghetti = witches' hair, that sort of thing)." RENATA

# 3

# Good games for great parties

There are so many excellent party games for all age groups, and so many different types to choose from, such as musical games, food-based games, team games, exciting games and calming games. You should try to pick a few from each section for a well-balanced party.

A lot of these games will work well for mixed age groups, which you are bound to have if siblings share a party, or if the non-party sibling has a few friends along. You may need to adjust things slightly in favour of the younger children, or have a run-through of the game first for their benefit. In any case, get the older ones to help run the games they have played before, but make sure that they don't take over.

## Games to get the party started

Party games can help shy children get involved with the party and are a very good ice-breaker when the guests don't all know each other already.

### The autograph game

At the start of the party all the children are given a piece of paper or card and a pencil. On the word 'go' they have to start collecting the signatures of all the children present, including their own. It is best to tell them how many signatures they are aiming for and have a checklist of all the names prepared before the party (and adjusted to take account of any last-minute no-shows). This is a good game for children aged six and up. Younger ones could still play, but they will probably only manage to collect first-names.

### Find the buried treasure

You need a globe, or a big map of the world, possibly from one of those giant, laminated children's atlases, a sealed envelope with the location you have chosen for the treasure written on a card inside it and a small sticky label with the name of every child attending. When they arrive, they each decide where on the map or globe to put their label. Later in the party you open the envelope, and the one whose name is nearest to the secret location wins the 'treasure'.

### A crafty way to start

A simple craft activity that everyone will be able to join in with, such as colouring in hats which they then wear for the party, is a good way for children to get to know each other if they are feeling a bit shy. Put some hat shapes cut out from card with a selection of crayons and felt-tips and decorations such as feathers and shiny foil cut-outs on a big table, and let the children join in as they arrive. If the party has a theme such as kings and queens or pirates then they can make appropriate headgear.

## Active games

### Treasure hunt

This can be played indoors or out and adapts well to a themed party. Hide things around the house and garden. The players either have to find all the sweets/coins they can or specific items such as cut-out pieces of a picture, hats or socks from a list of clues. They can either play individually or as a team. If you have mixed age groups, try to team older and younger children together to make things fairer. Make sure you have plenty of 'treasure' so that everyone can find something.

## Grandmother's footsteps

One person (usually one of the adults or an older sibling) is grandmother. They stand with their backs to all the children, who will be in a row up to 20 feet away. Everyone has to move closer to Grandmother very quietly when her back is turned. When she turns around anyone who she sees moving has to go back to the beginning. The winner is the one who tiptoes right up to her and taps her on the shoulder before she notices. They then become the Grandmother for the next round of the game.

## Tortoise or hare?

Before the party starts, make a list of different activities that have to be done either very quickly (hare) or very slowly (tortoise). For instance, fast hares might try writing their name, or ten things starting with a particular letter of the alphabet (paper and pencils handily provided for these tasks), hopping, skipping, jumping, stuffing pillows into pillowcases (probably not ideal for larger parties), finding three different things beginning with an s (you will have placed sweets, shoes, stamps and spaghetti, for instance, in strategic places beforehand, and may drop a few hints for younger children who don't have the alphabet at their fingertips yet). Slow tortoises can try eating a piece of chocolate, running round the garden in slow motion, moon walking, lying down and stretching. Lots of tortoise activities at the end of the game can be very useful if some calming down is called for.

## Traffic light actions

For this game green means fast, amber means normal speed and red means slow. Choose lots of different activities such as dancing, walking, jumping, skipping and hopping. Each activity has to be done on the spot, when you call it out, and at the speed indicated by the colour you call out at the same time.

## Follow my leader

All the children follow the leader (preferably an adult to get things started). They have to follow whatever the leader does as they move around – for instance, hopping, skipping, jumping, hands on head, silly walks, waving arms, being an animal, a fashion model, etc.

## Walking with binoculars

Mark a straight line on the floor with string or tape and get each child, one at a time, to walk along the string while they are looking through the wrong end of a pair of binoculars. See who can stay on the straight line for longest.

## Poor Kitty

Arrange the group in a circle with a blindfolded player in the middle. Get the players to move round the circle very quietly. The blindfolded player should touch a player on the shoulder, who should then say 'poor kitty' in a disguised voice, and imitate a cat's miaow. If the blindfolded player can't recognise the prisoner he releases him and the game goes on. If he succeeds the two change places.

### Changers

Everyone sits in a circle and one child leaves the room. Someone is picked as the changer, and starts clapping. Everyone follows what the changer does, and they all follow as quickly as possible every time he or she changes the movement – to arm waving, jumping, hopping on the spot and so on. The child who comes back in from outside has to watch everyone carefully and work out who the changer is.

## Team games

### Poker faces

Divide your players into two equal teams. Each team chooses its own name. Play some music, and when you switch it off shout out one team name. Members of that team have to make the other team laugh, smile or move any part of their face and anyone who does not manage to keep a 'poker face' gets a point. After a while, play the music again and then the other team gets a try. Go on playing, alternating the teams, for as long as they are enjoying it. The team with the lowest score at the end wins. This game works well for mixed age groups, if you make sure the teams are well mixed too.

### Balloon relay

Line the children up in two teams at one end of the room. Each team member in turn has to jump to the other end of the room and back with a balloon between their knees, before passing it on to the next in line. Anyone who lets the balloon escape has to go back to the start line and have their go again.

### Tennis ball twins

Two even-numbered teams get into twos who hold hands and face each other. The first two have a tennis ball put between their foreheads and have to run to the other end of the room and back without dropping it. They pass the ball on to the second two, and so on, until the whole team has had a go. The first team to get back behind the start line wins.

### Guess the feet

The children are divided into two teams and everyone takes their shoes and socks off. One team leaves the room, and the other team lies on the floor, under a sheet, with just their feet sticking out. Each pair of feet rests on a big piece of paper with a number on it. The other team comes back and they have to work out whose feet are next to which number, and write them down. When they have swapped, the winning team is the one with the most correct guesses when checked against the numbered list you will have made when each team lay down.

## Musical games

### Dressing up dancing

Choose five types of clothing – for instance hat, top, scarf, badge, apron – and make sure that there are enough for each child to have one of each. Put the clothing in the middle of the room, turn the music on and get the children to dance around. When the music stops you call out 'scarf' and they all have to grab one, put it on, and then dance while wearing it until the music stops again and they have to put on the next item you call out, until they are wearing all the layers, with a pair of grown-up shoes as the last thing (no more dancing once they are wearing their pair of too-big shoes!). Then they can do a little 'fashion' parade.

### Musical islands

This is easier to organise in a smallish room than musical chairs, but works on the same principal, and is particularly suitable for a pirates party. Cut out island shapes from newspaper, one per child, and put them on the floor. Each child stands on an island and when the music starts they dance around the room. You remove one island and when the music stops one child will be out. They get to pick up the next island to be removed, and so on, until the last two children are battling it out. If this is a success you could go on to old favourites such as musical statues or musical bumps.

## Food-based games

### The tasting game

Cut up pieces of food such as apples, grapes, bananas, carrots, chocolate, little squares of bread spread with Marmite or Nutella. Blindfold the players and get them to taste and try to identify each thing. The one who gets the most right should win some sort of little edible prize.

### The chocolate game

The children take it in turns to throw a dice. When someone throws a six they must put on a hat, coat and gloves and then try to eat from a big slab of chocolate, using a knife and fork. They can go on doing this until someone else throws a six, then it is their turn.

### The popcorn game

All you need for this is bowls of popcorn and straws. By sucking on their straw, each child tries to remove as many pieces of popcorn as they can. The winner gets a prize, and everybody gets to eat popcorn.

## Sitting down games

### Touch and feel

Take a box and collect up five or six contrasting items – for instance a grape, a pencil, a shoelace, a piece of Lego, a cotton wool ball, a toothbrush – and put each item in turn in the box and get the children to put their hand in the box and guess what it is. The last item could be some wrapped sweets for correct guessers to eat.

### The memory game

This is another one that can be adapted to go with a party theme – for instance, pirates or fairies, or creepy things for Halloween. Adapt the number of items to the age of the children, starting with about six or seven things for little ones. When all the children have had time to memorise the items one is removed, and they have to guess which one has gone, right down to the last one. The child with the most right answers wins a prize. Older children will enjoy the version where you place about 20 items on a tray, let them look at it for a few minutes, then cover it over while they write down as many things as they can remember. Let them swap papers to mark how many they have remembered, with prizes for the ones who have remembered the most.

### Forfeits

All the children sit in a circle around an empty bottle placed on its side. You spin the bottle around and whoever it is pointing to when it stops has to perform a forfeit, for a little prize. Make a list of about 20 forfeits beforehand, which can range from quiz-type general knowledge questions to actions such as hopping round the circle or doing ten star jumps or singing a verse of a song. Always have more forfeits than you need, so that you can keep the game going for as long as everyone is enjoying it. And make sure that none of the forfeits will embarrass the child who has to perform them – you don't want any of your party guests to be scarred for life.

## Calming down games

### The fame game

Make anagrams of the names of ten famous people (or three or four-letter animals for younger children) and write them in big letters on card. The children each have a pencil and paper, and see how many of the anagrams they can work out in a given time.

### Sleeping lions

The very best game for calming down. Everyone lies on the floor very, very still. If they move, they are out, but you may choose not to notice any movement for quite some time.

## Disco party games

### Disco dress up

Get some very silly glittery wigs from a novelty shop, and

some shiny scarves, pop star-ish hats, feather boas and other lurid accessories from your own guilty secret store or the Oxfam shop. Make sure everything is clean and tidy beforehand. At the party, put on the Abba, put the pile of dressing up stuff in the middle of the room, and when the music stops everyone has to dress up for a showing-off dance contest.

### Limbo dancing contest

You could get two older children to hold a thick rope about four feet apart for this. They start with the rope quite high, so that everyone can dance under it easily, then gradually lower it a few inches each time until it gets really difficult to dance under it, at which point a winner could easily emerge.

## Tips for choosing games

★ Get your child to help you plan the games. If they think something will be fun, their friends probably will too. By the same token don't push for things that you think would be great if your child is doubtful. When it comes to their own age group they probably know best.

★ Be age appropriate. Younger children can't concentrate or sit still for very long, so keep things simple and easy to understand, older children will like brainteasers and quizzes, memory games and charades.

★ If you are having a themed party, pick a few games that can be adapted to fit in with your theme – for instance you can pin a tail, or something, on almost anything, and pass the parcel forfeits can easily be adapted to a theme.

★ Plan more games than you think you will need. It is always better to have too many than not enough and it is great to be able to move on quickly if things are losing their fizz.

★ Be strict with yourself and if you can tell that a game is not going well, or that the children are getting bored, then cut your losses and go on to the next one as quickly as possible. Keeping children happily occupied is the best way to keep them under control.

★ If you get trouble, keep things moving and go on to another activity. Don't be afraid to be bossy with them.

★ Have a variety of types of game – active, calming, team, memory and so on, rather than sticking to just one category.

★ Have all the games set up and ready before the party and make sure you are clear on how the games will be played.

★ Have a list of the games with a clear running order, with some very calm ones towards the end.

★ Label all the bits and pieces with the name of the game they are for, in case someone has to take over from you in running the games. For the same reason, label any prizes that are for a specific game.

★ If any of the games depend on music being turned on and off make sure you have a tape recorder/CD player to hand that will do this, and check the batteries as well.

★ Have a few games where everyone gets a little prize. They can be the same sorts of item that you put in the goody bags, but put into a lucky dip so that prize winners can pick their own.

★ Get some inexpensive fake medals on ribbons to dish out as prizes for sporty games. These are available by mail order (see 'useful addresses') – or you could use chocolate coins instead.

★ Always have some extra prizes to hand in case you play extra games or have more than one winner, or decide to play a popular game more than once.

★ If the party is going to be outdoors make sure you have a few games that could be played indoors as well.

★ In elimination games, find something that the children who are out can do, such as keeping an eye on the game. Especially important for the first child who is out, who might be given a special job, such as being in charge of the music.

★ Keep the games short and lively for three year olds and under, who have a very short attention span.

★ Save the very best game for last so that you end on a high note.

# 4

# Catering and cakes

You can go to too much trouble when catering for children; they probably won't appreciate masses of home cooking. Rule one is that only a minority will eat the sandwiches, rule two is that they are all much too excited to sit down for long and will start running around again as soon as they have a piece of cake in their hands. The cake is very, very important, but more as a symbol than a foodstuff. A lot of children don't even finish their piece – its arrival signals the end of the meal and time to get back into action.

★ The most successful party food for a younger child is simple, child-sized and can be pretty healthy (with the possible exception of the little sausages, still de rigueur after all these years).

★ It is surprisingly easy to get children to eat some fruit and veg along with the other party food if it is small-sized – cherry tomatoes, grapes or strawberries – and looks pretty – carrot batons with dip on a nice plate. When the children are old enough to be safe with cocktail sticks, fruit kebabs are a huge hit. Thread different coloured grapes, strawberries, blueberries and anything else that looks pretty onto a cocktail stick. Any age group will like these.

★ For older children, it is usually just pizza, pizza, pizza.

★ A word about allergies, which are ubiquitous these days. Food, particularly nuts, can cause problems. If, as the party giver, you have any worries in these areas, it is a good idea to check with other parents before the party. Otherwise it is probably safe to assume that a parent who knows their child has a problem will take their own precautions and let you know before the party starts.

★ If you decide to give everyone a slice of that abandoned cake in their party bags do wrap it securely in foil. Otherwise your carefully sourced and wonderfully cheap party bag presents will emerge covered in crumbs and icing and will not be appreciated as they should. Personally, I would not bother.

## Drinks

★ To cut down on spills, juice boxes are a very good idea.

★ Do avoid cans of fizzy drink for as long as you can possibly withstand the pressure from your children. If not, someone who doesn't normally drink sweet fizzy drinks will drink three, get all hyped up and the whole thing will end in tears. If, eventually, you do have to succumb, the fun-size cans will avoid a lot of wastage and spillage.

## Cakes

Simple ideas are best. You need a cake that you have made before and know will turn out successfully, but in an emergency you can always improvise. I once had to plunge a Barbie doll, legs first, into the middle of a tall sponge cake, spreading her skirts out to cover the gash in the sponge, because of my inability to conjure up a fairy cake out of thin air. Nobody seemed to notice particularly, but with a bit of forward planning you can avoid this type of fiasco.

★ You want it to taste nice, and be appealing, so don't go mad on lurid coloured icing. A friend once made a very fancy cake with a vivid green layer. Some bright spark said it was probably poisonous, so none of the children would eat it.

★ Make the icing layer thin because it can be sickly, and a lot of children don't like it very much.

Even if you are not a great cake maker there are lots of ideas that you can put together using bought-in basics, or you can buy a ready-made themed party cake from the supermarket or cake boutique. Here are a few ideas for some assisted DIY.

**Train** A chocolate-covered swiss roll forms the engine, with two carriages made from another roll cut in half lengthways and filled with a cargo of sweets. Train funnels and wheels are made from cut-up mini chocolate swiss rolls.

**Castle** Ice cream cone turrets on the corners of a square sponge cake all covered with butter cream icing.

**Moon cake** Sherbet flying saucers for craters, covered in white fondant icing and some little space buggy toys.

**Treasure chest** A square sponge cake cut in half horizontally, and with one half standing upright behind the other. Cover the whole thing in chocolate icing and pile a treasure of gold and silver wrapped chocolate coins inside the casket.

**Snake** Just right for a wildlife party. Make or buy lots of cupcakes, ice them with butter icing in different shades of green and lay them out in a wiggly snake shape, turning the front one on its side to make its head, with eyes and a tongue made out of sweets.

# 5

# Four, five, six – a class act

Fourth, fifth and sixth birthdays are the nursery and primary school years when your child is most likely to want a big party involving the whole class, and so they are the years when entertainers, or at least very structured parties, are really important for your sanity and your child's enjoyment.

## Fourth birthday: easily entertained

This is a good age to have an entertainer. Most of the guests will believe in the magic tricks and laugh at the jokes, and it's an ideal time to have lots of easy games. But do alternate lively games with calm ones so that nobody gets too excited. Investigate whether your local playgroup hires out its premises at weekends. The advantage of this is a contained and fairly indestructible environment, with pint-sized furniture and jolly décor.

> "My four year old daughter had a little fancy dress party in the garden with hired-in tiny tables and chairs and an entertainer dressed as a fairy. I think that was the sweetest party ever, and I look back on it very fondly. "JULIE, MOTHER OF TWO

## Fifth birthday: fancy dress

You may well have the whole class to this one and, depending on when your child's birthday is in the school year they may still be getting to know each other, so it stands every chance of being a pretty lively affair.

You could give fancy dress a try as this may be the last chance to get them to dress up before they get too shy, and at this age the boys will be quite happy to be cowboys or super-heroes.

★ Have a few spare bits and pieces of costume around for the refuseniks who wish they had dressed up after all.

★ Or you could create your own fancy dress party on the day. You can collect up lots of bits and pieces for a dressing up box from things you find around the house. Old hats, scarves and handbags make a start, and such essentials as cowboy hats, Superman ensembles and ballet tutus can be found fairly cheaply in good toyshops. Give them an idea for a play to put on with some parents as audience, and leave the rest to their imaginations.

"When my son was five I realised our cottage was quite unsuitable for a party for boys, so I hired a room in a local hotel that had a really good, safe grassed area. The boys were each given little plastic swords – relatively fragile, so that they couldn't hurt themselves – and that encouraged lots of imaginative games out in the garden. Often at this age they only need a bit of prompting for all the imaginative stuff to come bursting out. I gave them some ideas, but they got really into it themselves. I'm not a great cake-maker, but this time the birthday cake was a castle, which really worked, and the combination of the castle cake and the swords was enough to really stimulate their imaginations. With the added benefit that the plastic swords were the going-home presents instead of party bags this really was a great party, which was so easy to run."
ELIZABETH, MOTHER OF TWO

"My mum joined forces with my friend's mum for a double-whammy birthday when I was five. The theme was horses. We had miniature jumps set up in the garden, handmade rosettes complete with a home-baked horse-shaped cake. It was amazing." LIZ.

"My oldest son's fifth birthday party was a nightmare. His brothers were respectively two years and one week old, and we decided there and then that never again would we open our house to a dozen over-excited small boys. So we did a deal with the kids. In future they could have two or three friends for a treat each birthday (cinema, sleepover, or whatever they liked) and then we would have one big party for everyone in the summer. This meant organising only one big party a year instead of three, and we could do it in August (instead of January when two of the boys have their birthdays) so we could be outside, which is far easier to cope with. Each child gets the benefit of two events a year instead of only one. We now have a huge summer party every year with no limits on numbers for invitations (there's always a high fallout because so many people are on holiday in August, which is fine by me) and everyone is happy." RONI, MOTHER OF THREE

## Sixth birthday: parties for the whole class

If you have the entire primary school class to this one an entertainer will be worth every penny, otherwise you will need to think of enough activities for non-stop action. As they get older the advantages of not being at home for the party can outweigh all other considerations. Marauding groups of excited six year olds may not be just what you want in your house. This is where village halls, sports centres, Scout huts or dedicated party venues really come into their own. The good thing is that children this age will be concentrating so hard on the party that they will neither notice nor care if the surroundings are a bit battered around the edges.

"When my son was six, we hired a church hall for his party. I ordered 20 helium balloons and drove them, with great difficulty as they filled the whole car, over to the venue. I tied them to each child's chair whereupon they were immediately untied by the guests. Unfortunately, the hall had an extremely high ceiling and we spent most of the party desperately trying to retrieve balloons before they ascended to the heavens. The boys threw food and heckled the poor entertainer but otherwise a good time was had by all." VICKY, MOTHER OF THREE

"For my sixth birthday I had a wicked party at a place called the Pirates' Play House. It is a big room in the sports centre filled with a massive kind of climbing frame with platforms and slides and swinging ropes and ball pits, and I had all the boys from school. The really great thing is that you and your friends go in there on your own and you can run around and muck about and the grown-ups are outside. After a while we came out and had tea, and then we all went back in again until it was the end of the party. We didn't need an entertainer or anything." HENRY

"My friend always has the best parties. When we were five and six her parents hired the local babysitters to come and help at her parties, which we all thought was much better than other people's parents, as they were much more cool. There would be a different activity set up in each room and we went around the house doing all the different games and things. The best one was in the conservatory where you were given a slab of cake to decorate with multicoloured icing and little silver balls. There was a prize for the best one, and we all got to keep our own cakes at the end." RUTH

# 6

# That's entertainment

When you are looking for a party entertainer, always go on personal recommendation if you can, but if that really isn't possible then take up references. A good entertainer will be able to provide you with contact numbers of satisfied customers. If you don't want to be the mum in floods of tears in the kitchen while a grumpy man with a dodgy beard runs through some tired magic tricks then you have to be sure of what you are booking. After all, a bad entertainer is just as expensive as a good one.

Most of the entertainers who have been working professionally for a while have things like the CRB (Criminal Records Bureau) check. People can usually check on an entertainer's website for recommendations from happy clients. If the entertainer operates under a character name, such as, say, 'Happy the Clown' then they may well be part of an organisation that sends out several people operating as the same character, and standards may vary. If a particular one has been a hit at parties you know of, it is worth trying to get his services. Parents should think about booking a reputable professional entertainer at least two months ahead, especially for a party at the weekend. Someone who is free at short notice might not be such a good entertainer.

★ Try to meet your entertainer beforehand to talk through what you want, and get to know them a bit.

★ If you can't get a personal recommendation ask around at your local school or playgroup, but don't book an entertainer that the whole class has seen a couple of times before; the children will get bored if they know the whole routine and some little fiend will delight in spoiling the tricks.

Entertainers don't all provide the same things and it is worth checking beforehand so that you know exactly what is on offer.

★ Will the entertainer organise games as well as provide a show, and if so, will they provide prizes?

★ Is the show geared to your child's age, with activities that are right for the age group? You may want to check exactly what the show comprises.

★ Will the entertainer give going home presents? It is worth bearing in mind that these may be pretty minimal and you should not really depend on them to keep the children happy.

★ Do they stay for the whole party, and if they do, will they expect to be involved during the tea, or do they have a break then? You may find it preferable to take over yourself during tea.

★ Do they bring a helper with them? If not, you will need reinforcements.

## Party professionals

### The face painter

"If you have a party theme it is a good idea to ask your face painter to organise a few pictures around the theme for the children to choose faces from." Elizabeth Scott has been painting children's faces for many years and has lots of ideas that will help to make this very popular aspect of many parties run smoothly. "You have to spend a bit of time with each child to find out what will appeal to them. If they don't want their face painted I might paint something on their hand or their arm, or just do a little decoration on their face so that they all feel part of the party. Pirates are very popular at the moment. The girls can be mermaids or sea horses and the boys can be fierce. If a child doesn't want the whole thing you can just paint on a bandana around their hairline. You can usually send a child away with something that they feel good about and that is the whole point really.

"One problem that face painters often have is that mothers can be a bit optimistic about the time it takes to get the faces on in amongst the games, the food and everything else. If the party is for two hours and they are having tea, games or other entertainment it can be pretty difficult to get 20 children's faces painted in the time. Rather than end up with disappointed children who don't get their faces done until the very end, when nobody will see them, it is really worth a mother who is giving this type of party thinking about hiring two face painters for a shorter time at the start of the party."

## The traditional entertainer

"When you have seen a professional entertainer in action the difference between someone who is just blowing up a few balloons and telling some jokes and the real thing is phenomenal," says a spokesperson for Smartie Artie, possibly the longest established children's entertainers in the UK. "A good entertainer will be able to enthral the children for the whole two hours without repeating any of the same material.

Smartie Artie covers a whole range of magic, jokes, fun and games and the show is geared to the age of the children. After all, you need a very different show for three and four year olds than you do for six and seven year olds, and they are experienced with all age groups and know what works."

This is a brand that has been going for some 42 years, and is mindful of having a reputation to protect. Prospective Smartie Arties are rigorously trained and are interviewed carefully at the outset to see if their personality is right for working with children. "We still have one of the almost originals. Smartie Artie number two is still working, and is now performing for the grandchildren of the people he first entertained. We pride ourselves that a high percentage of our work is recommendations and personal requests for a Smartie Artie who has been seen in action. We cover the whole country, even abroad, and including some very grand households indeed.

"Recommendation is definitely the best way of choosing an entertainer, otherwise it is pretty much a shot in the dark. It is so awful if you get a bad entertainer, and even some of the dodgy ones aren't necessarily cheap. If you are spending a fair bit of money you want to be sure you are getting your money's worth." [**www.smartieartie.com**]

## Animal magic

When you ask children to think of their most memorable party it is surprising quite how often it turns out to be one featuring wild animals. It is clearly unusual enough to find yourself draped in a live python for it to stick in your mind, and I have certainly never forgotten the sight of my six year old daughter, in her very best party dress, carrying a tarantula in her hands. These parties, run by people who care for their animals and are very knowledgeable about them, are educational and fun, too.

Nick Spellman, aka AnimalMan, offers a heady mix of magic, comedy and exotic live animals that can be handled by the children. He specialises in birthday parties for four to eight year olds, and operates in the South East, though he can make recommendations for similar entertainers in other parts of the country. His parties include birds of prey, spiders, scorpions, lizards, a snake or two – including a big python – a chinchilla, hedgehog, meerkat or skunk. The birthday child is always his helper, and children can touch some of the animals.

One of his main tips for successful parties is to make sure that he can be there half an hour early to get set up. "Children are never fashionably late. You should always have something to engage them with from the start. From about ten minutes before the official start time I always try to be in the situation where I can take the early arrivals and get them involved in something, which builds up as the other children arrive and avoids any shy-making moments." [**www.nickspellman.com**]

Designed for real wildlife enthusiasts, Animal Encounters is perfect for groups of up to 15 older children (aged nine and over) who want to find out more about the natural world. Birds, insects, a chinchilla, a fruit bat, snakes, even an armadillo, are part of the experience. There are also combinations of curious animals, entertainment and magic for the four to eight year olds. [**www.impeyanparties.com**]

## Useful tips from the entertainers

★ Tie a bunch of balloons to the door or gate so your house is easy to find.

★ Clear away distracting or potentially dangerous toys from the garden if the party is to be out there.

★ If your entertainer is mixing magic with games and competitions get the children to sit on the floor where they can see better and are easier to keep an eye on than when they are sitting on chairs.

★ If you are having face painting, give the artist a quiet corner away from the main action if you can, with a table and two little chairs the same height.

★ Put all the presents your child is given safely away in a big box or bag to be opened after the party, when you will be able to make a list of who has given what for the thank you notes.

★ If the party is after school always feed the children a glass of water and a biscuit before the party starts to give them an energy burst that will help them to hang on until tea time.

★ Remind any parents who do stay that it is only fair to the children to keep quiet while the show is on.

★ Save the balloons, squeakers and blowers for tea time, and then collect them up after tea so that they don't distract the children while your entertainer performs.

★ Tie balloons up out of reach, don't leave them loose on the floor if you don't want the children to go into a popping frenzy. Helium balloons left on the ceiling with strings dangling can be very distracting for children. It is best if they are firmly tied to going home bags or in groups on the table.

★ Remember party poppers are essentially fireworks and can

burn small children. They should always be supervised, not just left loose on the table.

- ★ If you can, have the tea in a separate room, and never serve ice cream or sweets during the show unless you want sticky little fingers wiped on your carpet and furniture.
- ★ When possible, get parents who arrive early to wait to pick up until the end of the performance, as it is very distracting if children have to be hauled out just before the end.
- ★ Keep the family pets in another room. Parties can make pets over-excited, and some little children are afraid of animals.
- ★ Don't forget to offer your entertainer some food – or at least a cup of tea.

Watching a good, experienced party entertainer doing his or her stuff for a group of enraptured children makes you appreciate just how hard they work – and just what a great investment they can be when you have a potentially unruly group of over-excited children on your hands. A good entertainer can deal with the one child (and there always is at least one in every group) who refuses to play along with the magic or join in the games, and may even be able to make them lighten up and enjoy themselves. However, do your utmost to avoid entertainers who are no longer at the top of their game.

> "The first time we hired an entertainer, when our daughter was four, we looked in the directory and ended up with a chap who obviously didn't like children very much any more, and had a load of mothy old games and tricks that he fished out of a battered briefcase. Fortunately for, us, most of the children at the party were quite new to the entertainer thing: if they had been a bit older and more party-wise we might have had problems getting them to sit still and watch." NEIL, FATHER OF TWO

You want the entertainer to be in charge and keep everyone under control, but there have to be limits.

> "My brother once had a party where we hired this slightly past-it entertainer who actually sent a boy out for talking at the same time as him. Not fun." JENNA

It can happen that your entertainer is grumpy, or hopeless at magic, or is a DJ with all the wrong tunes. You can do your best to research it beforehand, but what do you do if the entertainer can't keep the children entertained? Really, your only option is to cut their part of the proceedings tactfully short and do your best to take over with some games, otherwise you will have party mayhem on your hands.

# 7

# The great party bag debate

Children don't generally want a single tasteful little item wrapped in tissue paper at going home time; they prefer *proper* plastic party bags with sweets and *proper* plastic toys in them. These days the stakes have been raised to a point where parents can feel pressured into spending anything up to £10 on each bag. If you have even ten children at the party this adds up to silly money.

Do check the whole thing out with the party child first. If giving their friends something you approve of – a tasteful little present/organic party bag full of wholefood 'treats'/whatever – is going to make your child miserable or embarrassed then that rather defeats the object of having a party in the first place. However, spending a fortune may be going to make you miserable, in which case you should try to do something about it.

We do seem to have got into a bit of a state about this, and it is wrong to blame children for expecting party bags when they have grown up going to parties where they are the norm. At the same time it is curiously reassuring to discover how fond children are of the cheap plastic nonsense that is traditionally the staple ingredient of the party bag. It certainly doesn't seem to be the children who are agitating for the expensive party bag fillers.

## How to fill a party bag without emptying your wallet

- ★ Try to get all the mums in the class to agree a price ceiling for party bags. That should cut down on the price-sensitive one-upmanship – you will be left competing to see who can be most ingenious on a budget, which is probably healthier.
- ★ Make sure that you put the same things in all the bags. Nothing causes more trouble than an unequal division of the spoils.
- ★ Museum shops are a good place to hunt out inexpensive little presents.
- ★ Don't put face paints in the bags – sometimes they can cause an allergic reaction.
- ★ Don't forget to include a bag for the party child. It is surprising how much they care about this.
- ★ Always make up a few spare bags in case you acquire a couple of stray siblings at the party.
- ★ Avoid party bag contents that make a mess – glitter is a particular no-no. Other parents will not be thrilled if the back of the car is covered in sparkle and cake crumbs on the way home from the party and somehow bits of glitter always elude the vacuum cleaner.

## Alternatives to party bags

- ★ As an alternative to a party bag, and a good party game in its own right, save lots of copper coins and hide them around the house for a treasure hunt. The children can take home their loot at the end.

- ★ A cone of home-made popcorn is an economical end-of-party treat.
- ★ Fill a clear plastic cup with colourful sweets (and maybe one little party present) and cover it with brightly coloured cellophane tied up with a ribbon bow. Use lots of different coloured cellophane or tissue paper and the whole thing will look great.
- ★ Younger children love things with their names on. A huge cellophane-wrapped decorated biscuit, with the child's name written on it with an icing pen is bound to be a hit.
- ★ A little plant in a pot or at the right time of year a hyacinth bulb with a glass growing jar, a mustard and cress kit or anything that they can watch grow will make a real change. A flower pot and seeds seem very appropriate if you have given a garden party.
- ★ Match the going home gift to the party theme if you have one – for example modelling clay or pencils and drawing pads for an arty party.
- ★ A lucky dip for a single present each at home time instead of a bag adds a final burst of excitement to the party.
- ★ For a beach party, buckets and spades with nets and things for playing in the rock pools and so on during the party add to the fun of the day as a great alternative to a party bag at the end.

## What children think about party bags

"What's in the bag doesn't matter *so* much – but there has to be a bag or you feel a bit cheated. It's nice to have a normal bag, with some sweets and some plastic-y toys – the sort your parents will never buy you because they say they are rubbish." PRUDY

"I always look forward to the party bag, but it is not the main thing about the party. That would be sad. Party bags do mean that it isn't quite such a big deal when the party ends as you still have something to look forward to, even though they usually have a bit of cake in them that breaks into crumbs all over everything by the time you get home." HENRY

"Some of the things in the bag can be a bit boring – and it is really annoying when they break straight away – but I would be really surprised if I didn't get one." WILL

"I got a book in a party bag once. I never read it, but I did think it was a nice thing to be given. The best party bags have a bit of variety – some sweets, a toy or two. They may be things that you forget about the next day, but you love them at the time." PHIL

"I love party bags full of chocolate and sweets. Once we were given bags that just had one felt tip pen in them and I thought that was really bad." JENNA

"My mum got some pretty fans from a Chinese shop for our party bags, and my friends loved them and took them to school afterwards, so I felt really pleased. I think one pretty thing like that, as well as some sweets, a piece of cake and something like crayons is perfect." RUTH

"I've never been to a party where there wasn't a party bag, so I think we do expect them really. I don't really mind what is in them. Even though they are full of rubbish and you usually eat all the sweets on the way home and have forgotten about the bags by the next day, they are nice to have." FLORENCE

"I think party bags are totally lame. Soggy pieces of cake (I don't even like icing!) and silly plastic things. The good thing is that two of my friends have mums who are artists so they make really cool stuff to go into party bags. One of them prints her own paper, and binds notebooks, so we get little ones in our bags, which is cool. The other arty mum made these really pretty mirrors one year, and we each got a little one with our name on it. Very lovely." JENNY

"My sister got a goldfish as a going-home present at a party once, and my mum was really fed up about it." RICKY

## What parents think about party bags

"The sad thing is children start to expect them and feel peeved if they don't get one. Sometimes that is the thing that they are really waiting for. One nice idea was a mum bought a load of jolly paperbacks, very cheaply, and when they left they all had a book and a piece of cake. On the whole they seemed pretty pleased with that. There seems to be a lot of competition these days which is all about what you spend, then it is not about the children but impressing other adults, and parents feel under so much pressure. One really good idea was a box of little magic tricks and jokes, which was not expensive to put together but gave everyone hours of fun afterwards." CLAIRE, MOTHER OF TWO

"There is a lot of one-upmanship about the bags and some parents do go over the top, but I can't be bothered with all that personally. I tend to fill them up with sweets and bits of nonsense and maybe one more expensive thing but if I can help it I don't spend more than about £4 per party bag, so I'm going back to a more traditional sweet-filled thing. My children are fine with that and I think their friends seem fine too. Perhaps I have given them low expectations. When you have already gone to quite a lot of expense then for 25 kids the amount you can spend on party bags can be a bit crippling. When they are competitive it is much more about the parents than about the children." MEMONA, MOTHER OF THREE

"I feel very irritated by the idea that children expect a party bag so some years I haven't given one and then disgruntled children asked where they were so it seemed to be absolutely expected. You can easily spend more than £100 which I think is ridiculous, but my children were really unhappy and embarrassed when we didn't have bags for people, so I think now I would always give something, if not a party bag." NAOMI, MOTHER OF FOUR

"In my experience if you try to do anything original or interesting with party bags the kids don't like it. They want what they are used to, and they are embarrassed if you deviate from the normal. Stick to the formula for the age group and they will be happy, and if that means plastic junk so be it." JUDY, MOTHER OF TWO

"I hate the load of rubbish you can spend a fortune on for party bags so I like to give them useful stuff like big wooden pencils, fun straws, useful things that they enjoy and I am happy to buy. You don't have to spend a fortune." MARIE, MOTHER OF ONE

"Party bags should be small when they are little and stop at 11. They don't need them at big school." JULIE, MOTHER OF TWO

"I think party bags are awful, but you have to have them. It is very hard when your children go to other parties and get them – you just feel that you have to do the same, so I bite the bullet and come up with the goods. I try not to spend too much on them. Children just want the due thing at the end of the party. It is bound to add up to at least a few quid per child, but if there is a class of 25, you can easily end up spending £100 on not very much. Using kids' parties for one-upmanship is horrible. Party time is quite stressful because you feel you have to think of something different that all their classmates haven't had before." JO, MOTHER OF THREE

8

# Seven, eight, nine – action packed

## Seventh birthday: expedition force

At around this age a lot of children go off the big, invite-the-whole-class type of party, so some sort of activity or expedition such as swimming, a picnic or a trip to the cinema or zoo, for a selected group of friends may be just the thing.

It is generally easier to have parties out of doors than indoors, and you should make sure you use all the natural advantages at your disposal. If you live near the sea then go for beach parties; if you are in the country, head for a local attraction; in most cities you are never too far from a park.

For any kind of excursion involving more than a couple of children you need the help of at least one other adult, particularly for places such as theme parks, where the children may not all want to do the same things all the time, and even practical things like organising trips to the loo can be a worry if they involve splitting up the group.

A **picnic** is a relatively hassle-free way to celebrate, and with warm, rainproof clothing does not have to be confined to the summer months (after all, when was July ever a guarantee of sunshine?). If you pick somewhere like a park, National Trust property or beach where there is a café not too far away then you have an inbuilt plan B if the weather turns on you. For plan C (storm-force rains or worse set in for the day) you may have to have the picnic at home, so lay in a few DVDs and indoor games for emergencies, but still serve the food on picnic rugs on the floor.

A **garden party or a barbecue** can be lots of fun for this age group, with the proviso that you have to have some way of keeping them dry if the weather turns terrible. It is worth investing in one of those cheap gazebos from a DIY store so that you have some shelter if it is only raining a little bit.

Barbecue food can be simplicity itself, and this age group is particularly easy to feed if you have plenty of hot dogs and burgers and keep them coming. You hardly have to do anything in advance, just chop loads of onions, sprinkle them very lightly with oil and wrap them in a tinfoil parcel that you can put on the barbecue. By the time you have cooked all the sausages and burgers the onion will be ready, for perfect hot dogs, and you can put the burgers into rolls with some salad for a healthy touch. Just don't forget the ketchup, and try to find an edible brand of veggieburgers or sausages if needed. For pudding, big yellow bananas barbecued whole until the skins are black all over taste really good. Just slit the skins, sprinkle the fruit inside with brown sugar and eat with a spoon.

## Good outdoor games for the garden, park or beach

### Water relay

Divide the children into two or three teams, each with a bucket of water, a large sponge and an empty one-gallon sized clear plastic jug or bucket. The buckets of water, with the sponges in them are at one end of the race course, with the jug at the other end, and the object is to be the first team to fill the jug with water using the sponge. The first player soaks the sponge with water, runs to the jug, squeezes the water into it and runs back to pass the sponge to the next player. This continues until the jug is full. You may find that a little food colouring in the jug will help the teams to see how much water they have got into the jug, and how far there is still to go. You could use a different colour for each team.

### Obstacle course

It is a lot of fun to set up an obstacle course in the garden, using what you find there, and if you can get the children to help you may be surprised at their ingenuity. A course could include crawling under sturdy garden chairs, walking with a ball between your knees, hopping along the length of a winding garden hose, crawling under a groundsheet or through an empty cardboard box open at both ends, throwing tennis balls into a bucket. Then get them to complete the course against the clock.

### Sack race

Preferably run this on a grassy lawn or sandy beach as there may be some tumbles. Old pillowcases will do for sacks. Each player should climb into the sack with both feet and pull it up high enough to hold onto the edges and then have a bit of a hopping practice before this hilarious race starts. Egg (or potato) and spoon and three-legged races are also a lot of fun.

### Beach relay

Divide into two teams, each with a beach ball and a beach bag filled with two flippers, a snorkel mask, a pair of large swimming trunks and a pair of sunglasses. Teams form two lines at one end of the course, with the beach bag full of things at the far end of the course. The first runner in each team has to run to the bag of items while keeping the beach ball between their knees. They then have to dress up in the beach items, then take them off and run back to give the beach ball to the next player. This goes on until everyone has had a turn. Small prizes to the winning team, who will deserve them after all that effort.

### Scavenger hunt

Make a list of outdoor things to find, suitable for the garden, park or beach and the season. For instance: three types of leaf, a daisy, a primrose, a conker, a pine cone, or seaweed, three different coloured pebbles, a shell. The child, or the team, that collects the most objects on the list in the time is the winner.

## Winter games to play outdoors

### Torchlight treasure hunt

Winter birthday parties tend to rule out the whole bouncy castle aspect of things, but there is still stuff you can do out of doors if everyone wraps up well. If you have a winter party children really enjoy an outdoor treasure hunt in the dark. Give them all little torches (which could then go in their party bags) and send them out into the garden to look for shiny sweets or something else that will show up in the dark. That works for Halloween parties as well.

### Firefly

Outside in the dark with their torches, three children are chosen to be the fireflies and are given a few minutes to hide. Then they have to keep flashing their torches on and off while the others try to find them and catch them when they run away. When someone catches one of the fireflies they take their place.

## Don't forget

- ★ Matches for the birthday cake – and some sort of wind shield to light the cake behind.
- ★ Something to sit on.
- ★ A black bag for rubbish.
- ★ A pack of wet-wipes.

> "My best ever party was at a forest maze. The cake was a totem pole of all different types of cake stuck on a spike, and we ate it inside a tepee we had built out of sticks." RUTH
>
> "Eight or nine year olds enjoy an element of friendly competition – it keeps them entertained. My daughter and her friends loved a treasure hunt in the garden when she was eight. All the party guests were put in pairs and there were ten clues to solve altogether, some were quite hard and took ages, some were easy, and we sent them all over the garden and parts of the house. When they got to the end they all got some 'treasure', which was a lucky dip with really good presents in it." NICK, FATHER OF ONE

## Theme parks

There comes a time when a day at a theme park is the dearest wish of most children, and the deepest dread of most parents. The great joy is when they are finally old enough to go on their own, or at least to go on the rides on their own, and you don't have to make any further additions to the collection of brave yet terrified photos of Mum on the runaway train.

### Theme park dos and don'ts

- ★ Have at least one adult with you for moral support and to accompany the children on the rides you can't face, until they are old enough to go on them without an accompanying adult.

★ Don't take too many children with you; it is expensive and also worrying keeping track of them.

★ Bear in mind that a lot of rides only let children on when they have reached a certain height, so the ones who have not grown as much as their friends may be left out and very fed up. Check beforehand if you can, and change plans if necessary.

★ Fix a meeting up point and make sure that everyone knows exactly where it is in case the worst happens and you get separated.

★ Trips to theme parks always seem to attract extremes of weather. Make sure you have sunscreen, lots of water for everyone to drink, and that they all bring some kind of waterproof top.

> "Theme park parties are generally great but I went to a stupid one recently. My friend had ended up with an uneven number of people so it was really difficult to all go on the rides because they are all for groups of two or four. Also, some people were really scared and didn't want to go on the rides, so the rest of us couldn't, so that was quite boring." SAMMY

## Eighth birthday: sleepover parties

Whether at the end of a party, or as the main point of the party in itself, children love having their friends for a sleepover. They have so much fun that it is almost worth the total destruction of your evening that inevitably ensues, and the fact that they will all be over-tired and over-wrought for the next few days. Almost.

## Sleepover damage limitation

- ★ Serve a big, energy-boosting breakfast in the morning and then make sure everyone gets picked up before tempers can get seriously frayed.
- ★ Don't expect to get much sense out of your child the day after a sleepover, which means they have to be held on a Friday or Saturday in term time so that there is time to recover before school.

"I really like sleepover parties but the one my best friend had this year for her tenth birthday wasn't so much fun. We were having a really good time dressing up, doing makeovers and eating take-away pizzas, but then my friend's parents wouldn't let us watch the film we wanted as it was a 15 certificate and they thought the other mums and dads would be mad at them even though we had all already seen it. Also, they made us go to bed quite early and kept telling us off if we were noisy, which was so annoying." GEORGIA

## Camping sleepovers

"Some of our best parties for our daughters have been camping parties and they work brilliantly. Our kids have summer birthdays and we have a big garden so we invite about a dozen children for a camping party. They come in the late afternoon and play loads of games in the garden. Then we make a little campfire and they sing campfire songs and toast marshmallows after tea. After a few more songs they get into their tents (we have two six-person tents that we put up, and one adult in each). The eight year olds like there to be a mum and dad around as they do get a bit more frightened in the night than the older children do. They have managed to stay out there all night, though I always have a back-up plan and have our loft room kitted out for them as well just in case.

"This sort of party works best for ten to eleven year olds who are probably at the ideal age. They get the flavour of camping in the garden but it is better than going away with a lot of them. We have lots of mats and sleeping bags so they are comfortable. The main problem is that it is weather dependent. If it is raining but warm, that's OK; the problem is if it is cold. Then it tends to turn into a sleepover in the house, which they still enjoy, though it is not such an adventure as the camping. We have huge problems getting them to go to sleep, which is what always happens with sleepovers, so you are giving back a limp rag of a child in the morning, but I have never found a way around that. They are always so excited that you know that that will be a difficult one, so you have to warn the parents that they will have a tired child the next morning. Our parties are always on a Saturday, so they have Sunday to recover.

"Other parents seem to be really glad that we do these parties as it lets them off the hook with their children when it comes to camping. I think camping isn't generally that popular any more. A lot of kids haven't camped at all when they come to one of our parties so they really look forward to it and the parties have all been really successful. It has the added benefit of being less expensive than other types of party we have done – and I would say more rewarding as well. You have to get loads of food, and, of course, you still have to have party bags.

"We often have an extra twist. One camping party was a pirate party. Everyone dressed up and we had arranged games for them with a race track sprayed on the lawn and very traditional games like a three-legged race, carrying a cup of Long John Silver's blood in a teacup (red dyed water), walking the plank (a wobbly plank over a paddling pool full of water), and lots of good games like that, with the camping to round things off." MEMONA, MOTHER OF THREE

## Nights at the museum

There are other ways of guaranteeing yourself a sleepless night in aid of the party. The Science Museum has been running its legendary Science Night sleepovers for groups of eight to eleven year olds for many years now, combining fun and hands-on learning with the chance to camp out for the night in very unusual places. Now other venerable institutions are letting their hair down and joining in with the all-night parties for avid pre-teens. These nights to remember tend to be so popular that you have to book up a long time in advance, so it is as well to plan ahead.

Science Night is an evening of well thought-out activities and hands-on workshops which take place in different parts of the museum after it has closed to the public, rounded off by camping in the Science Museum overnight. It's thrilling for children, if a little tiring for the escorting adults (don't expect to sleep much and take your own pillow and eye mask). All children must come to Science Night as part of an adult-accompanied group. The smallest group you can bring is five children and one adult. [**www.sciencemuseum.org.uk 020 7942 4747**]

There are four sleepovers a year when you can spend the night exploring the British Museum after dark. Getting involved in storytelling and craft activities before settling down to sleep among the mummies may seem a little creepy but only in a good way. If you huddle together and have plenty of midnight snacks, it should be fun. Access to the sleepovers is via membership of the Young Friends of the museum. [**www.thebritishmuseum.ac.uk 020 7323 8000**]

Sleepovers at the National Media Museum, Bradford, give parties of children (age six to 12, at least one adult per six children) the chance to explore the galleries after closing. You might meet a Dalek, watch an IMAX film and star in a radio show before bedtime. [**www.nationalmediamuseum.org.uk 0870 7010200**]

At the midnight ramble at the Royal Botanic Gardens at Kew eight to 11 year olds (one adult to four or five children) stay overnight in the botanical play zone and explore in the 300 acres of the gardens, searching for local wildlife such as bats, owls and badgers. They also get to experience tropical jungles and desert and play with a range of games and activities culminating in stories and marshmallows around the camp fire. [**www.kew.org 020 8332 5655**]

For something completely different try a Shark Slumber Party at the National Marine Aquarium, Plymouth, where guests aged five or over (in a minimum group of four to include one adult) get to sleep in front of the tank after an evening of movies and a midnight feast. [**www.national-aquarium.co.uk 01752 600301**]

At the Royal Armouries at Leeds, children's events include sleepover nights, which include games, a disco, and the chance to sleep in the galleries (a ratio of two to three children to one adult). [**www.royalarmouries.org 01132 201916**]

The whole Night in the Museum trend seems to be growing in popularity – it is worth checking with your local museums and galleries to see if they are operating anything along these lines.

"My Science Night sleepover party was great. It was for my ninth birthday, though we had to wait until quite a long time after my actual birthday for a date when we could go. It was a really fun way to learn about science because they taught us much more interesting stuff than we learn at school. My favourite activity was making hot air balloons out of tissue paper as my team's was the best and they looked really pretty and colourful. But the very best thing was staying up all night giggling with my friends and annoying the Brownies sleeping next to us." PRUDY

## Ninth birthday: sporty parties

What is it with boys? At this age they simply crackle with energy. But misguided missiles though they are, boys enjoy an activity party of any kind. At this age lots of girls enjoy things like football, too. If your local sports centre or swimming pool lays on parties this can be a very easy option. They should be able to give you information on the possibilities for sports parties – and it may be possible to hire coaches to help with games. Trampolining parties are possible at some venues and are always popular, and centres with a climbing wall may be able to offer climbing parties, too.

★ Keep an eye out for anyone who really isn't enjoying the games – they could help you to get the tea ready.

★ You really can't be too careful at a swimming pool. Restrict the number of children you invite, have lots of adults who will swim, too, and make sure the pool has lifeguards supervising.

★ They all love a trampoline. You need to make sure you don't have big, boisterous children bouncing with the littler ones and it all needs to be very well supervised. Trampoline-type parties can be a great way of using up some of that energy, but you must keep an eye on them all the time. The same goes for bouncy castles.

★ A lot of football clubs offer parties on their hallowed turf –

maybe your nearest, or the one to which your child has pledged eternal allegiance, is among them.

"I couldn't recommend ice skating parties for boys. Within five minutes of the start of my son's party two boys had bumps the size of eggs on their heads, and I thought it would be a miracle if we got out of the rink without an ambulance. I spent the whole time worrying. Girls tend to concentrate more on getting things like skating right, boys just go for it, with potentially disastrous consequences." JANE, MOTHER OF THREE

"Activity parties are great. For my last one we booked the local sports centre where we had football with a coach, and then swimming and then masses of food." PHIL

"Our best ever party was for my son's eighth birthday, when we had a Jaws party at the swimming pool. The invitations were adapted from the film poster and I managed to make a shark-shaped cake. We hired a local pool with a water flume (and, fortunately for my peace of mind, a lifeguard in attendance) and the catering was courtesy of McDonald's, which was, of course, a major favourite with all the boys. They all loved it, and it really wasn't all that much work for me." ANGELA, MOTHER OF TWO

"I had a miniature golf party for my twin boys when they were eight, and they still talk about it. I always think you should make the most of what you've got when it comes to parties and it helps to have a big straggly garden for this sort of thing; you wouldn't want to ruin an immaculate lawn. We sank biggish coffee tins into the ground all around the garden, making the most of the natural obstacles, and borrowed golf clubs and balls. At that age they quite like arts and crafts and getting involved with the planning, so the boys made and decorated the flags for each hole on glossy card. The invitation was a diagram of the shape of the garden with the holes marked. We had about 15 friends plus some parents and a lot of dads joined in with the golf. If you are a single parent, as I am, you need to get another adult or two to help you. Then you do have to spend a bit of money on stuff for the dads, like wine or whisky, and a bit of grown-up food, though they all seem to wolf down sausages anyway." SALLY, MOTHER OF TWO

"Go-karting with my nine year old son and his friends was a nightmare. The place was tedious and gloomy and there was a lot of hanging around in between their turns when they all got bored and restless, and it was hard to think of anything else they could do but just hang around and watch. If we did it again we would take far fewer boys so that they could have their turns together and then we could leave and go somewhere nice for some tea." BILL, FATHER OF TWO

"When I was ten we went to a place where you could do dry slope skiing. We took eight friends and my sisters. The boys all thought it was great, but my sisters didn't enjoy it much." ED

## Craft activities

Just for a change you could try a craft party – jewellery making or pottery painting for girls, something like T-shirt or mug painting for everyone. This sort of party works well for groups of like-minded children from the age of four or five upwards, with the crafts obviously getting more complicated as they get older. However, it might not be the best choice if you have any lively boys on your guest list who don't like to sit down for too long. I remember once picking up a car-load of mutinous six year old boys from a party at a craft centre which had been given by a girl in their class. The main thing they had had to do for two hours was paint a plaster cast of their initial. The girls loved it and made their initials look very pretty before going on to other activities. The boys just used one colour, and as soon as the initial was covered they mucked about for the rest of the time. This might not be what you want, so choose your guests carefully.

With the right personnel these parties work for lots of age groups. You can buy all sorts of kits to make a home-based craft party a fairly easy option, either concentrating on one activity or having a choice of several on offer – such as necklace beading, painting, decorating things – appealing to different age and skill levels. This sort of party can be quite inexpensive. If you go to places such as Hobbycraft you will find loads of ideas. [**www.hobbycraft.co.uk 0845 051 6522**]

★ Pick the sort of thing that your child enjoys doing – chances are their friends will enjoy the same things.

★ It may be a good idea to offer a selection of things to do.

★ Have a couple of extra projects around for quick workers and try to have something completely different to do lined up for those whose attention starts to flag.

★ If you have the energy to supervise operations this is a good alternative to booking parties at craft centres and you have more flexibility to find the sort of thing that will really appeal to the children who are coming.

★ To make it easier for you it is probably best to start this sort of party at four or older, though some three year olds might enjoy it too.

★ If you don't fancy organising something like this at home, you can go out to a pottery painting workshop, where they specialise in organising parties, or you may have somewhere locally dedicated to arty/crafty parties, or someone locally who will come to your house and organise something like jewellery-making or T-shirt painting.

Make things easier for yourself if you are organising a craft party for the younger end of the age spectrum by getting a kit from **www.petitartisan.com**. They have a selection of craft party kits, each designed to entertain six children who can make a bead bracelet, paint and decorate a jewellery box or a pirate chest, paint a dinosaur or assemble and decorate a wooden race car. The projects are suitable for ages three to four upwards and for boys and girls and the children get to take home what they have made. If you are having boys and girls to the party you could invest in a couple of different activities to keep everyone happy.

"On my son's fourth birthday it was raining so we couldn't go outside as planned and I quickly had to think of something else. My son was really into astronauts and space at that age, so my husband nipped out and got some space pictures photocopied and the children coloured those in as their first activity. I got a load of craft paper and cut out lots of stars and moons that they could make up into hanging mobiles for their rooms and they decorated those with glitter and stickers." CLAIRE, MOTHER OF TWO

"My cousin's jewellery-making party when she was seven was a really good idea. It was in her kitchen, around the big table, and there were loads of different types of beads including some with letters on so you could spell out your name. We were allowed to make three things each. I made a matching necklace, bracelet and clip-on earrings and then the woman in charge attached the fastening to them. It was really good because then I had some nice jewellery to take home with me. The next year my cousin had a T-shirt painting party, where we were given a choice of stencils to colour in and loads of sparkly glitter and sequins to stick on. That was great, too."
KATYA

"We took our daughter and a group of her friends clay painting for her ninth birthday, which was fun, but a bit regimented. The kids have to do the painting at a certain time, then have tea, then go. Some of the slower, more meticulous girls were hard pushed to finish what they were decorating in the time. As a party it was very easy for us, because all we had to do was hand the money over, but we did feel that the children might have had more fun and freedom of choice if we had organised something similar at home." MARGIE AND JIM, PARENTS OF ONE

## Cookery

Cookie Crumbles is a company that operates very popular cookery parties for children aged from four to14. There are different themes and menus for the different age groups: four to seven year olds might make and eat goodies on an animal theme, seven to tens develop their cooking skills preparing a themed meal such as pirates' bounty, space odyssey or disco divas, while 11 to 14 year olds will enjoy the sophistication of preparing and eating food from a dinner party menu. [**www.cookiecrumbles.net 020-7622 4448**] There may well be something similar on offer in your area, or brave parents with indestructible kitchens might try to dish up something like this for themselves.

"I feel that the fashion for big expensive parties is slightly over. Most people now seem to be inviting smaller groups of children to do more interesting things. For my daughter, who is ten, we have just had a party where they were taught some Chinese cooking, which they all thought was completely brilliant." LOUISA, MOTHER OF FOUR

"When I was nine I had a party where a really nice lady came to the house and taught me and five of my friends to make pasta and a sauce to go with it. We made the pasta by putting the flour right on the kitchen table and mixing an egg in it, and then we rolled it out and cut it in a special machine. Then we made a tomato sauce which was really nice and cooked the pasta. It was great making our own food, and I was able to tell my mum a couple of things about cooking pasta right that she didn't know." GEORGE

9

# Party politics

Running a party can be a minefield of modern etiquette and you can fall right in before you even realise that there is a potential problem.

## Sharing a party

Joint parties can be fraught with pitfalls for the unwary. If you share a party with another child in the same class at school it only really works if you are inviting the whole class – when it has the great benefit that you are splitting the cost with another family. Otherwise you get into the thing where the children have different groups of friends and they may not all get on, or a small number of children in the class don't fit into either friend-group and don't get invited, which is just plain mean.

When you are planning to share a party with another family it is important that you establish at the outset exactly who is doing what and providing what, so that you don't feel hard done by and don't end up doing all the work, unless of course that is what you prefer.

One area where you should establish *exactly* what you are each going to do is the catering. I remember one shared party we had where the other mum said that she would bring sandwiches. She meant exactly that – two very beautifully prepared rounds of sandwiches, for a party of 20 ravenous girls. We had to dash out to the shops for extra supplies to avoid mass hunger. Another time a rather unworldly dad who volunteered to be in charge of soft drinks only got as far as the expensive local off-licence, rather than venturing to the supermarket and buying in bulk, so we ended up paying about double what we should have done.

Make sure you all (including the children who are having the party) agree about invitations, contents of party bags, decoration and all the other details before you start.

Ideally share with other parents who will do as much work as you do. Beware of Alpha Dad who is much too important to help with keeping order or clearing up and concentrates on networking with the parents who come to pick up their offspring, or Clipboard Mum, who runs round writing children's names down and ticking things on lists rather than actually doing anything useful.

## The guest list

As the children get older you may invite only some of the class. At mixed schools this is less complicated, (boys probably won't want to go to girls' parties at some ages and vice versa), but at single sex schools who is and isn't invited can get tricky. One good solution, from a mum whose children are at a school where classes are so small that omissions are very noticeable, is to make a rule that if your children don't want to invite the whole class then they have to invite less than half, so that the ones not invited are the majority.

## Discouraging parents from staying

If parents stay the children often don't enjoy the party quite so much. As the children get older parents tend to relish the couple of hours' free time offered by a party and leave them to it. If you don't specifically invite them, parents generally won't expect to stay at a party after the children are about five, although if you offer a drink at picking up time you may find them hard to budge. Whole family mixed age group parties can be enormous fun, but they are something else entirely.

# 10

# 10 plus – coolhunters

## Tenth birthday: murder on the dance floor

At this age they love a disco. You can either hire a DJ (the advantage is they will have lights and maybe karaoke) or do your own with all the children's favourite music, and some games or competitions. Really between the ages of ten and 12 or so this is all they will want: it all gets more tricky once they are teenagers and you have to police the parties much more carefully. All the problems start when they want to have alcohol at the parties, so make the most of the time when they are still young enough to be told what to do.

★ Stock up with lots and lots of water to drink.

★ Enlist some adults and older siblings to help you supervise.

★ Have some games or dancing competitions to make it more party-ish. This age group won't want to just dance all night.

★ Make sure the DJ is aware of what kind of music your children and their friends actually like. This is much more crucial now than it ever was when we were young.

### Stretch limo

Grown-ups may find them unspeakably naff, but hiring a stretch limo for her party will gladden the heart of a girly ten year old girl. My god-daughter and nine of her friends all dressed up to the nines (with her father 'supervising') and went off for a fabulous hour, cruising around town, with balloons and fizzy drinks in the limo, stopped to take movie-star type pictures of themselves with the limo, and were then deposited at a pizza restaurant to calm down a bit over some solid food. Magic.

"For my tenth birthday I had a simply amazing makeover party. My mum let me have my friends round to perform all sorts of hideous beauty treatments and make-ups on each other. We all felt so grown up, and at the time the Spice Girls were still our complete style icons, so there was plenty of inspiration. My next door neighbour's daughter worked for a beauty company so we had loads of free samples of stuff to use. It was really fun, and my mum made sure that there was plenty of make-up remover on hand so that nobody went home looking too scary. The only problem was the incident with the bronzing pearls and the carpet … it never quite recovered. And that was the last party I was ever allowed at home." JENNY

"Our very best party was a disco for ten year old girls. They really loved it and danced for hours. We ordered in pizza, which is what they all seem to prefer at that age, and I am particularly keen on the fact that you can serve it in the boxes so there is no washing up afterwards." SARAH, MOTHER OF FOUR

"My favourite ever party that sticks in my mind was a Spice Girls party when they were at their peak, which was when I was nine. Everyone came as their favourite Spice Girl, and there was Spice Girls everything, everywhere and we all thought we were in heaven." FLORENCE

"Between the ages of ten and 13 I shared a disco party with another boy from school. We were at a mixed school and invited the whole class, and it was a lot of fun so we did it every year until we all left that school. Our parents hired a church hall and a DJ. The best year was when we had a really good DJ who had a karaoke and did lots of games, and got to know all our names. The worst one was when we had a DJ who played the wrong stuff and didn't seem to be very interested in what he was doing." GEORGE

"We took 20 assorted nine to 13 year olds to Singalonga Sound of Music which was really good fun. Another good theatrical party was a children's theatre workshop where they wrote their own play and the parents came back to watch the performance." JULIE, MOTHER OF TWO

Part 2

# Ages 11 to 21

# 11

# 11th to 13th birthdays – the in-betweenies

Too old for toys, too young for the unbridled horrors of a teenage disco, all growing up at different rates, this age group is often happy with friends, DVDs and a sleepover, or a meal at a restaurant with *no adults* (you pick a suitable venue, drop them and pick them up and, of course, pay.) Actual parties may call for a bit of ingenuity, but with this age group can be great fun.

## Murder most horrid

You can buy a ready made plot for a murder mystery party in a box, but if you, or a friend, have a flair for creative writing, you could have a really memorable party like this one:

> "When my daughter was 11 she had a Murder Mystery party which was enormous fun. A family friend wrote the story for her and, as they were studying the Victorians at school, that was the theme. Everyone came in costume, there were 12 girls – all of whom we knew would enjoy that kind of thing, and they were all sent their roles in advance. All the guests were particular Victorian characters such as Lewis Carroll, Charles Darwin, Charlotte Bronte, Charles Dickens and Sherlock Holmes.
>
> "The murder victim, feared newspaper columnist Jasper FitzDemon, never appeared in person. He was in his study writing articles with

his poisonous pen and was found murdered offstage. Charlotte Bronte did it, because she knew he was going to ruin Emily Bronte's about-to-be-published Wuthering Heights with a bad review.

"It was easier to make up the plot because we used well-known historical characters, real and fictional, to hang the story on. Everyone had to have a motive, a secret, and be seen by other characters in suspicious circumstances. For instance, Grace Darling was seen by Sherlock Holmes leaving FitzDemon's study, and then he was seen by another character doing something unlikely and suspicious.

"The back story was that the house party was taking place at the house of the Party Girl. She had two older siblings (a real-life touch) and was due to inherit money that she planned to use to open a home for wayward girls – a fact that she had to keep secret from the evil siblings. We wove the real family in with the historical guests, and her parents were part of the plot and had secrets too, just pitched at that age group, so it was all about snobbish aristocrats and secret love affairs. There were some great scenes. Lewis Carroll and Charles Darwin got together and dressed as characters from Alice in Wonderland to scare Jasper FitzDemon, who shouted 'Carroll, this time you have gone too far'. People who heard this would not know if he was shouting at Lewis Carroll or the servant girl called Carol.

"Everyone was sent their bits of the stories and directions on what to do in advance. There were three scenes: dinner, later that night and the next morning. It was a lot of work establishing who was where, when and with whom, but a lot of fun, too, and the girls were just the right age to act it all out and make it a magical party. One of the adults was the policeman who questioned everyone, because it was better to have someone slightly outside the party in charge. The solution had to be something we could all have

guessed if we were smart enough, as Dorothy L. Sayers once said, so the information had to be there for everyone to see if they were looking. It turned out that Charlotte Bronte's alibi was totally fake, and everyone knew the true facts without necessarily realising it."
PATTI, MOTHER OF THREE, AND WRITER GABRIELLE

"When my twin girls were 13 we had a Quasar party for them. The twin thing really came into its own then as they could each have a team. They are robust, sporty girls and their friends are, too, so it was great. I always found that anything where they could have a team really worked." SALLY, MOTHER OF THREE

"Go-karting is terrific for in-betweenies. We had a party for a group of 11 year old boys and they all had lots of fun. It was the sort of party where nobody gets left out. At that age they have very short concentration spans and so just drove the go-karts for four minutes at a time and watched each other go round in between. The short time slots meant that there was a good balance between watching and taking part, so no one had time to get bored, which I think they do if they have to wait a whole 15-minute session before their turn. You need to limit the number of children so they aren't hanging around for too long, which just makes them a bit fractious, while being on the track for the solid 15 minutes is quite tiring for them. Far better to split up the time into short bursts, with copious amounts of food to follow." SARAH, MOTHER OF TWO

"When I was 13 I went to a boy from school's bar mitzvah, which was a 1950s-themed bowling party. It was amazing. There were hairdressers doing '50s-style hairdos for everyone, a T-shirt printer making a T-shirt with your face on it, non-alcoholic cocktails and an ice cream van parked outside just for us." FREDDY

"This year we are doing a paintballing party for our 11 year old daughter, who is a bit of a tomboy. When we sent out the invitations we included the form explaining that they may get bruises and nowadays you have to get the parents to sign something saying that they are happy for their child to attend. They all wanted to go! The worst paintballing injury I ever heard of was when two dads took a load of kids for the day, and one reverted to the school bully he obviously was once upon a time and shot the other dad in the face. The kids were all fine, however. Moral: pick your support carefully." STEVE, FATHER OF TWO

12

# 14th to 17th birthdays – don't try this at home

From the age of 13 or 14 onwards, your children will want you to go out and leave them to it if they have a party, but it is probably not in anyone's best interests for you to do that. Depending on the sort of teenagers you have, the sort of friends they have, the sort of friends their friends have and how much you prize your fixtures and fittings, you may choose to have the party away from home. If not, it is as well for you to stay put – even if you have to hide upstairs. Your teenagers may actually be very glad you are there.

Countless parents will have had the experience of hiding out in an upstairs room, with the dog and all the strong liquor in the house, listening anxiously as a tide of destruction rolls beneath. It is an ugly job, and can be uncomfortable if you have had to move most of the furniture upstairs as well, but it has to be done.

Really, the best advice is that if there are going to be more than about ten guests, if alcohol has started to rear its ugly head, if the party consists of boys and girls, don't have the party at home unless you have lots of support, or you live in a big empty field. Most parents are united in the view that this lot are too young for alcohol, though some of the teenagers will go to great lengths to disagree.

If you have a party full of hyped-up 14 year olds they will want to behave like the bigger teenagers, but your job is really to stop them. You will need a full set of adults to keep an eye on things.

> "My daughter shared a 14th birthday party with two other teenagers and we insisted on a guest list so that we could keep an eye on who was coming in. Of course they all arrived at once so we had to take a certain amount on trust. All six parents were there to keep a pretty beady eye on things and every time the youngsters tried to sneak out for a cigarette we had to get them back in .We felt that we had to control all the entrances and exits. At that age you are responsible for them and you can't just let them slope off. It is best not to have any alcohol at all for this age group." JANE, MOTHER OF THREE

The much-needed silver lining is that this does not have to be an expensive type of party. You need lots of water, and fizzy drinks, but not much food – pizza and chocolate brownies will just about cover it – and bring out all the Christmas fairy lights for decorations.

## Ideas for teenage parties

A responsible older sibling who can keep an eye on things with a couple of friends if the party child is at the stage where the merest whiff of a parental presence is social death will be worth their weight in gold. Though if things get out of hand they will still want your help, so don't be too far away.

Roulette parties have a certain sophistication for the 15 to 17 year olds, with someone a little, but not too much, older as croupier. After that age they tend to go off that sort of thing a bit, although James Bond-themed 21sts do seem to be in vogue.

"When my daughter was 17 she didn't want to organise a proper party, so I arranged a pink dinner party for her and six friends. The menu was prawn cocktail, salmon, and then raspberry pudding, with pink 'champagne' to drink. I got it all ready and then cleared off and left them to it, and they had a great time." CHRISSIE, MOTHER OF ONE

## Party horror stories

The horror stories do not lie. If your child misguidedly posts party details on one of the social networking sites then you have no control over who might turn up at the party. If you find out that this is what has happened then you should seriously think about getting some experienced door security.

### A visit from the police

"I was due to be away for a few days, and at the last minute my 15 year old son asked if he could have a couple of friends to stay to keep him company. While I was away I just had this gut motherly instinct that all was not well, so I rang my neighbour and asked her if she could just go and check my house. I was just waiting for her to call back when the phone rang. But it was my son, and he said that someone wanted to speak to me. He handed the phone over and someone said 'This is the police'. My naughty son had invited about 30 people round and someone had complained about the noise. My neighbour had arrived to find three policemen there. The police were really lovely and said that all the young people were behaving pretty well, if noisily. Apparently the kids were all very polite and left when they were asked to. However, when I got back, it took me three days to get the house back to normal, although my son swore he had cleaned up. Moral of the story – trust your instincts, if in doubt don't leave your teenage son on his own, but if you do, my experience is that the police are very good at dealing with the aftermath." SOPHIE, MOTHER OF THREE

You have to be aware that a bit of drink at this age is inevitable, but it is probably going to be much better if it is under your control. This is not always possible, however, and often it is the guests rather than your own child who cause the problems.

## Secret drinking

"My son's very last birthday party in the house was when he was15. There won't be another, though it really wasn't his fault. After a lot of discussion we had agreed on small but face-saving amounts of alcohol – a tiny amount of champagne and some beers, but not many. However, one of his friends smuggled in quite a lot of vodka in lemonade bottles, the kids got really drunk and a couple of them were sick, some furniture got broken and I had a really anxious time of it. Afterwards I felt that the other parents were blaming me, but by the time I knew what was going on the damage had been done. My son didn't really want to join in on the vodka thing and he had a horrible evening worrying about what was happening in his home while not wanting his friends to think he was being pathetic. It is impossible to over-estimate the effect of peer pressure when it comes to this kind of drinking, and however vigilant you are you can have problems with this age group." JUSTIN, FATHER OF ONE

## Placating the neighbours

"When my son was 16 we had a party, which mercifully mostly took place in the garden. I woke up to the sound of someone being sick on the patio. When I got downstairs, as well as the obligatory stolen traffic cone in the kitchen, I was also greeted with the sight of a large 'for sale' sign in the middle of the lawn. The flowerbeds were awash with cans and bottles which had been smuggled in to bump up alcohol supplies and we had to spend the next day placating neighbours, particularly the one whose 'for sale' sign had mysteriously disappeared." VICKY, MOTHER OF THREE

# 13

# Facts on drink

## Drink dos and don'ts for teenage parties

★ If you are serving alcohol for older teenagers make sure that there is plenty of food to sop it up with. The consensus among parents seems to be that sixth form parties are the right age to start having alcohol, but limited amounts, preferably with the bar supervised by an adult.

★ Try to stick to beer or wine. Use the smallest glasses (probably plastic) that you can get away with, and the lowest alcohol content.

★ Steer clear of spirits and cocktails. "The whole atmosphere of a party changes if you bring spirits into the equation," says one professional party planner. Weak Pimm's is popular, and makes a reasonable alternative.

★ Have limited amounts of alcohol and lots of water and soft fizzy drinks available. They won't all want to hoover up lots of booze.

★ If any of your young guests are seriously the worse for drink you should see it as your responsibility (unfortunately) to make sure they are kept an eye on.

## Drink driving

One of the things that worries parents the most, and frankly with good reason, is the thought of inexperienced young drivers on the road and over the drink driving limit after a party. By far the safest way is to encourage young people to use other forms of transport after a party, or to stay the night, and not to drink at all if they plan to drive. They should be aware of the UK legal limit of 80 milligrams of alcohol in 100 millilitres of blood – roughly four units of alcohol maximum for men, and three units for women. But there is no fail-safe guide for how much you can drink and stay under the limit.

It is important to remember that one unit of alcohol does not necessarily equal one drink. One unit is equivalent to 10ml of pure alcohol. A rough guide is that:

- ★ 1 pint of strong lager = 3 units
- ★ 1 pint of ordinary lager, bitter or cider = 2 units
- ★ 175ml glass of wine = 2 units
- ★ average glass of champagne = 1.5 units
- ★ small glass of wine at around 11-12% alcohol = 1.5 units
- ★ average can of beer or lager, approx three-quarters of a pint = 1.5units
- ★ small glass of wine at around 9% alcohol = 1 unit
- ★ 1 alcopop = 1.5 units
- ★ 1 measure of spirits = 1 unit
- ★ lagers and ciders sold in bottles are usually stronger than those sold on draught. Find out how many units of alcohol are in the bottle by reading the label.

Police can breathalyse you if they suspect you have been drinking too much before driving. The test estimates the concentration of alcohol in the blood. If you fail the test you will be charged, and the breath test stored as evidence. Failure to give a breath test is an offence. Penalties for drink driving are a ban, fines and points on your licence.

Young drivers setting off the morning after a 21st, for instance, should know that on average the body breaks down alcohol at a rate of one unit per hour, depending on numerous factors such as weight, sex, age, metabolism, stress levels, amount of food eaten, medication taken and type of alcohol consumed.

## Drinking and the family

Many people are surprised to discover that it is only actually illegal to give alcohol to children under five, but sensibly most children do not get their first taste of alcohol until much after that, except perhaps for the occasional sip of champagne at a wedding.

Between the ages of around 12 to 14 some children will encounter alcohol at parties, sometimes with ghastly, bilious consequences, which may have the advantage of putting them off for years. The best thing parents can do is to talk about alcohol and what it can do, and stay calm if their children have been drinking without permission, on a single occasion, while explaining fairly forcefully why it is not a good idea.

Generally parents seem to agree that it is OK to serve moderate amounts of alcohol (but not spirits) when the children are 16, but preferably not before. Of course, a lot of teenagers think this is very lame, so compromises do have to be reached as most parents would rather have this age group where they can keep an eye on them. There are always going to be some households with a more laissez-faire approach to teenage drinking, which is one of the reasons why it is still a good idea, even when they think they are old enough to do what they like, to know where your children are going to be and who they are going out with.

## Drinking and the law

★ It is illegal for children under five to drink alcohol.

★ Police can confiscate alcohol from under-18s if they are drinking in a public place.

★ Under-18s are not allowed to buy alcohol from off-licences or in the bar area of pubs, clubs or any licensed premises, so anyone who sells to them is committing an offence.

★ Young people may only be allowed in to certain popular pubs and clubs on production of ID to prove that they are 18, and are unlikely to be served without ID in many places. This means that if an 18 year old has a birthday party in the upstairs of a pub or in a club, any friends who have not yet had their 18th birthday cannot legally be served alcohol.

★ Sixteen and 17 year olds can be given beer, cider or wine with a meal in a licensed establishment if they are with an adult (18 and over).

★ The police advice is not to drink alcohol *at all* if you are going to drive.

## Why your party needs one stone-cold sober adult

At least one of the responsible adults present must go totally on the wagon for the evening. Just in case you have to make a mercy dash in the car or deal unexpectedly with the police (and, for all sorts of reasons, this seems to crop up more than you could expect) a clear head is essential. Look forward to the great big drink you will clearly need – and deserve – when it is all over.

### Talking to the police

> "We wanted security for the evening of our son's 21st party and decided that as masses of people were staying and we had every expectation that the party would go on very late it would be best to have someone through the night and pay extra. He did deter a few random would-be gatecrashers during the evening, and as it turned out we were really glad of his presence later. There was a bit of irritating but harmless horseplay with some leftover food and a boy, who we later discovered had a history of behavioural problems, got out of hand.
>
> "There was a fight that escalated and the boy said he had a knife. At this point the security man fetched me and the other mother and tried to calm the boy down. We weren't having much success and he went and got into his car and tried to drive out, but the security man had very sensibly blocked the exit on the basis that there were people sleeping in their cars and he wanted to minimise the possibility of intruders from the village green. The boy was given the choice of going to bed and calming down or we would have to get the police. Then he ran away and we had no choice but to get the police, as he was in quite a state by that time. I was so glad that I had not had anything to drink all evening so I was able to talk to the police. I was told that they will not take a witness statement from

anyone who has been drinking as this could later be challenged legally." SUSAN, MOTHER OF TWO

## Emergency off-licence dash

"We thought that everyone would go for the fizz, at the 18th/21st party we gave for our children, and stocked up accordingly, and then on the night we discovered that most of the 18 year olds preferred beer and we had under-catered disastrously on that front. By then it was almost ten o'clock, and thank goodness I had had nothing to drink so I was able to jump into the car and hurtle into the off-licence just as they were closing. We sneaked the beer in without anyone noticing, and all was well. It really is worth one adult deciding not to drink for the duration as you never know what may happen." LEO, FATHER OF TWO

You could buy a breathalyser and get the drivers to use it before they leave, although for guidance only as commercially available breathalysers are not guaranteed 100% reliable. Remind them that they will lose licence points if they are caught with too much alcohol in their blood and don't let any one drive if you have the least doubt about their sobriety. It is far, far better to pay for a mini-cab or drive them yourself.

# 14

# 18th and 21st parties – this time it's serious

## Advice from a party planner

So here you are, on the home straight after all those years of children's birthday party planning. But this is the big one and you may want to call in some help from the professionals. Even if you don't, you may find some expert advice useful when you are formulating your own plans.

Party planner Christine Jones gives us the benefit of her many years of experience when it comes to planning 18th and 21st birthday parties. She stresses how important it is for parents to be involved in exactly what is going to happen:

### Numbers

"Eighteen year olds can't be left to decide how many friends to invite. You will end up with far too many. Parents need to be there for the evening; that is very important. Parental presence curtails any excesses. Our experience is that if parents go out that is when it can get out of hand – the house can get trashed, the neighbours upset. Subtle supervision, on the other hand, gives it the feel of a family celebration. Younger siblings can enjoy it and you get a nice family atmosphere as opposed to a rave-up. Inviting a few special adult friends changes the atmosphere for the better, too.

## Food

"You need food that fits in with the age group. Something that soaks up the alcohol like chilli and rice or a hog-roast or barbecue, is vital. Don't stint on the food. It doesn't have to be expensive. Whether it is a buffet or a sit-down it needs to be substantial – not just a few bowls of nuts and crisps. The best buffets for this age group tend to offer a simple selection of a few things – for instance chilli or hot cooked ham, rice or potatoes, maybe a vegetarian lasagne and a green salad, lots of bread and then cheese and one type of pud served in industrial quantities, rather than lots of little things.

## Drink

"Venues that have a bar where over-18s can go, with no food so all they are doing is drinking and dancing, can be very troublesome in this context, and you may want to steer your children away from this choice if you can. No venue should be serving drinks to under-18s, so they will need ID and then you will have no control over what they are purchasing at the bar, and there can be a heavily competitive element to bar drinking. You don't want complaints from the venue or other parents the day after.

Parents have to plan responsibly. At home or at a party you are organising you can stick to beer and wine or punch and you more or less have control over what they drink. Serving spirits is a recipe for excess. Parents are sensible to stick to beer/wine/soft drinks. If you put thought and planning behind the drink provision you will have less potential for trouble on what can be a long evening.

## Guest list and party plan

"You need a proper invitation list and to know how many people are coming so that you can plan properly. It is just no fun if you have too many people for the space, it is hot and crowded and nobody enjoys it. For a big party you need a plan. You need to know how many people are coming. If you have a band you need to know what time they will start and finish, and what time you expect the event to end. For the neighbours it can help if you can tell them what time you expect the music to be turned off. Send them a note letting them know about the party, even invite them in for a drink in the early part of the evening rather than ignoring them. If they are involved and informed they will often be very helpful, allowing people to park in the drive and so on, and it is far better to have a helpful neighbour than one calling the police at two in the morning because of the noise.

## Themes

"Lots of people like smart black tie or serious fancy dress such as 18th century, Gatsby or James Bond for 21st – they all love to dress up. If you have a big budget it is easy to make a party work, but you can still have a really good party on a restricted budget, you may just need to plan a bit more carefully. Themes like cowboys, pirates or tropical island, are all very popular and can easily be adapted to different budgets.

## Catering tips

"People tend to think that they should go for finger food because it will be cheap and cheerful but, in actual fact, by the time you have bought or made all the bits, which can take a vast amount of time, something like a chilli and rice or a curry, which are good options for this age group, can be a lot more cost-effective. With this kind of food it is very easy to add one dish that will be suitable for vegetarians or those on particular diets.

"Otherwise, you might think about a barbecue with really great burgers and sausages, which is the kind of food that age group loves anyway. None of these ideas has to cost a fortune but they're all great for soaking up alcohol and giving energy to the kids who are going to be partying until the early hours. You can hire in six-foot gas barbecues rather than dad slaving over the charcoal and the food can be ongoing throughout the evening. Something that you may be surprised to find is a really cost-effective option is a hog roast. This seems really special but is surprisingly economical because one pig can easily feed 100 people really well. All you need is to find a local butcher or farmer who does them and on the evening the roast can be carved to order and looks spectacular. It can work out at as little as £4.50 to £6.50 per head. As you can spend a lot of money on nibbles without realising this might be a much better option and it also looks a bit theatrical, which adds to the occasion. It can become a focal point of the evening."

All this proves that you don't have to be having salmon in a marquee for your party to be great. You don't even need the marquee. You can put up a few gazebos in the garden and still have a great time. As Christine says, "This option can look quite spectacular if you have fairy lights and tea lights in little jam jars all over the garden. With a bit of effort anyone can create a great atmosphere without spending a lot of money. In the winter lots of farmers let their barns out for not very much and again that can be great fun – you can have a barbecue or a spit roast and a barn dance.

"As professional party planners we help people who are on any kind of a budget. Parents need to get away from the idea of doing something in the house and then finding that poor old mum and dad are the ones doing all the work, panicking, rushing around opening packets of crisps all night and then doing all the clearing up. If it is in a venue or in the garden or a barn or village hall it leaves the house intact and you don't have to worry about the place being wrecked."

## Security

Experience has given Christine strong views on this. "With all the horror stories we have always suggested that if people are having a biggish party at home then it is money well spent to have proper security at your house. No matter what the size of the house, if you have someone on the gate or door just checking who is coming in and looking at their invitations, that gives an element of organisation and control to the people who are arriving so that subconsciously they may think that they had better behave themselves, and it also stops gatecrashers just wandering in. When people do have a party at home, 18 year olds all talk to each other and say they know where there is a party on and before you know it your house is absolutely heaving. If it is invitation only and you have someone on the door, that can work really well. Our security doubles up as helping people park their cars, tactfully stopping them from getting back into their cars and driving if they shouldn't and generally being a responsible face. It gives an extra element of safety. No parent wants people driving when they shouldn't. Security can have a word with the parents in charge."

## Chill out and calm down

"At formally catered parties these days it is recommended that clients should have a 'chill out' area where coffee and hot chocolate and soft drinks are served so that it is not all alcohol related, and if you are organising your own party you could try to factor in this idea. Quite often by one or two in the morning people quite fancy a cup of tea and a restful sit down. Another thing you can do is to serve something like bacon rolls at about 1am. This interrupts the flow of drinking, changes the pace and calms the party down a bit."

Among the many parties Christine has organised, some stand out. "My personal favourite was actually a few years ago – a 21st for a young lady who is very much in the public eye. It was a Gatsby theme, so everyone was dressed up in 1920s clothes and looked stunning. It was in a marquee and was very well organised. Everyone threw themselves into the theme and what I liked, and have always found to be true, was that because people were dressed up they behaved much better The live band and the food were within the theme and we worked with the birthday girl and her mum on this. It was done on a budget and it all worked perfectly. They hired in and borrowed props and everything looked fantastic."

If you are having a theme the advice is to try to get people involved in it and have food and props that fit in. "It is better to have a theme and stick to it. I think that a casual Western evening with a barbecue or something like that is much better than just having people turn up for loads of drinks and a crisp. If it is too open-ended with youngsters it can be a disaster – they need parameters."

## The canapé option

Whether catered or home-made, the important things to consider when serving canapés are quantity and variety. Caterer

Lizzie Harris stresses the importance of a regular flow of food. "You need canapés to be served at the rate of three to four per hour, and the longer the party goes on the more food you need to have, with plenty of snacks and crisps at fixed points as well as the food you hand around on trays. If you are following the canapés with a main meal then you probably need a total of four or five different canapés. For a drinks party evening with no other food you would probably want to serve ten to 12 canapés per person, but maybe have double quantities of six rather than 12 different ones, which might be a bit much.

"Choose a selection of hot and cold things, not too outlandish for this age group – they tend not to be wild about raw fish, for instance, but enjoy Chinese and Asian influenced things, sausages, of course, fried things and anything with a potato. You need a few fairly heavy things so they can fill themselves up a bit, to soak up the alcohol, and don't forget a few vegetarian options.

"If you don't have much space you should get as far as you can with the preparations in advance so you cut down on the cooking smell on the night. If you are simply heating things up at that stage, so much the better.

"Make things look attractive with fun plates and big platters, and decorate them with flowers for a really exotic touch. Always have someone to help with the handing round; you will get very stressed if you try to do it all yourself."

### Top ten easy canapés

1. Cocktail sausages, drizzled with a little honey and sesame seeds, served hot.
2. Smoked salmon blinis (mini blini bases from the supermarket, smoked salmon, crème fraiche, mock caviar, dill) prepared ahead and served cold.
3. Mini bruschetta. Bases made ahead or bought, covered with an assortment of pate, tapenade, houmous, cream cheese, and topped with olives, sun-dried tomatoes, salami, anchovies, gherkins, arranged in a selection on a big platter.
4. Mini Peking duck pancakes, assembled in advance.
5. King prawns in a coriander, lime garlic and olive oil salsa, made ahead and refrigerated until needed.
6. Something in breadcrumbs – prawns, chicken or fish goujons, served hot with mayonnaise or chilli dipping sauce, or tempura vegetables, which are popular with everyone and a chance to serve something hot for vegetarians.
7. Mini pizzas (or large pizzas cut into small pieces) served hot, again with a vegetarian option.
8. Prawn toasts (bought) served hot.
9. Fruit kebabs.
10. Strawberries dipped in chocolate.

## Marquee hire

People usually have a pretty clear basic idea of what they need and how many for but they don't often consider factors such as wind, which is the main scourge of the marquee business, as

Luke Craze, who runs a marquee hire firm in the South West, points out. "If you are on an exposed site with high winds you will have real problems, so I always recommend that people have a contingency plan for weather emergencies. It is only realistic in this country. Another factor that people don't always consider is whether there is enough grass to anchor the marquee. People measure the space, but if you have a four-metre wide marquee you need at least six metres of width to fit it in with the ropes, so you have to be realistic. A narrow town garden is not going to be ideal for any kind of traditional marquee for this reason, so you may need to consider something with a fixed frame, or see if the neighbours mind having your fixings in their gardens. If you have lawn surrounded by concrete there may be no way of fixing the pegs.

"People need to think whether they want everyone to be able to sit in the marquee, and if they are having food served at tables and/or a dance floor. You can fit more people in with rectangular tables in a rectangular marquee, but people always seem to have round tables in mind." Choosing flooring for your marquee is also an issue, particularly if you are having dancing. "I suggest that people cut down on any worries about drink driving and put the kids in the marquee to sleep after the party for 18ths and 21sts," says Luke, "so they need to think about flooring that doesn't let water come through, and it may be well worth hiring some Portaloos, if you don't want everyone traipsing through the house."

You need to book your marquee pretty far ahead for particular summer and bank holiday weekends. Early July and early September are especially popular weekends for people who are trying to make sure all their friends are not away on holiday and they do get very booked up, so you should try to get things ordered up to a year ahead, bearing in mind particular festivals and other annual events in your local area, which may lead to a heavy call on marquees.

## Party planning check list

Whether you are having a black-tie marquee bash or a barbecue in the garden:

★ As soon as you have decided on a date send out 'save the date cards' to the people you really want to be there. This may seem unnecessary, but the year everyone is 21, in particular, seems to get really crowded with parties, and you don't want half your child's best friends to be committed somewhere else.

★ Have a plan, and a guest list, and keep them both up to date as they inevitably evolve over time.

★ Work out your food and drink beforehand down to the last detail. If you have groups of different ages coming, think who is likely to drink what.

★ Always over-cater. It is miserable to run out of anything while people still want it. And order masses more fizzy and still water than you think you could possibly need – you can always use it up later.

★ It goes without saying that you will factor in some special catering for vegetarians and those whose diets are restricted by religion. Some extra special salads, tomato or onion tart, cheeses and smoked salmon cover a lot of bases, but in my experience the difficulty is stopping your other guests wolfing down all this food as well. If you are having a buffet it might be as well to label at least the vegetarian options, and point your guests in the right direction when you first start serving the food.

- Clear up all bits of food, crisps and so on, by around midnight. People won't eat them but it will seem irresistibly witty to chuck them around, and clearing up the next day will be even more of a nightmare. Anyway, you will probably serve some kind of a breakfast/ bacon roll-type thing later, if you have lots of people making a night of it.
- Tell the neighbours if they are likely to be affected by noise. It is a courtesy to drop a little note in a couple of days before explaining about the party, what time you expect the music to stop and perhaps inviting them to join you for a drink early on in the proceedings. This is a nice thing to do and on a purely pragmatic level, it makes it harder for them to complain about the noise later on.
- Consider the option of security, or failing that, co-opt some dads or big brothers to put on the yellow waistcoats and be in charge of parking, if you need it, or on the door checking admissions.

## Fancy dress

Dressing up is just as popular with this age group as with the younger children, and some of the party themes we have heard of are really ingenious.

- Dress up as the year the party person was born. Currently the excesses of 1980s fashion, available at an Oxfam shop near you, are causing much mirth and ribaldry amongst the 18 to 21 year olds. Just wait and see who'll be laughing in 20-something years' time.
- Dress up as something or someone with the initial(s) of the

party giver(s). For instance, A and E gives you Adam and Eve, Andy Warhol and Edie Sedgwick, Accident and Emergency.

- ★ Dress as the time you happen to open the invitation – if you open it at 18.30, dress as a person from the 1830s. Lots of scope for futuristic costumes for anyone who opens their invitation much after 8pm.
- ★ Your childhood ambition – lots of superheroes and ballerinas at this one.
- ★ Pirates (yet again), Wild West, football, cartoon characters, Gatsby, James Bond … all keep cropping up.

"I went to a great 18th birthday which was a treasure hunt round London. We all met at Waterloo Station where we were put in teams of three and given a series of questions and tasks. We had to pick up things like a matchbox at the Oxo tower, and so on. In amongst the other clues there were ones that sent us to meet up at a succession of three different pubs, and at each one a member of each team was given a costume. By the third pub we were all dressed up and each team had to work out from the costumes what their theme was (they were all Shakespeare plays) and you got a prize if you guessed it." TOM

"We had a combined 18th and 21st for our daughters with a pirate theme, which worked really well. We had a camp fire in the garden and a marquee decorated with palm trees with a star cloth all over the inside of the tent so it was black and the palm trees really stood out. We had white tablecloths with mirrors on the top and helium balloons attached for the table numbers – only a few because otherwise the numbers took off! We had a holey old rowing boat which has been in the garden for ages as an ice bucket, and lots of plastic skulls and rats around the place.

"What impressed us all were the costumes. Everyone went to huge trouble – lots of it Johnny Depp-inspired. There were masses of great flouncy shirts and waistcoats and cummerbunds. Lots of people put their own costumes together but a few hired stuff. The great thing about a pirate theme is that you can easily improvise. Lots of the girls wore white dresses with waistcoats, fake tattoos and make-up for the boys and loads of cutlasses.

"We had (weak) Pimm's and canapés before, then steak and chips and a meringuey pud, served at tables in the marquee, with wine and beer to drink. All formality stopped by pudding time – they still can't sit still for all that long. We had booked a jazz band, who turned out to have a combined age of about 4,000, with an antique lady singer in a tight dress. As it turned out they were no good for dancing, so we cut to the disco until 3.30 am. I rather wish I could have got a personal recommendation for the band or have booked someone we had seen before.

"We had bacon rolls and a birthday cake moment at 1am, then lots of people sat around the camp fire on hay bales, toasting marshmallows. Quite a few of the boys took an interest in looking after the camp fire. I would say that you should always appoint someone reliable to take charge of something like that. We served lots of croissants at about 5am, then more proper breakfast at 9 or 10. I was perhaps over concerned about transport, but my daughters were glad I organised it for their friends. We had a fleet of mini buses to take them all back to the nearest mainline station. The party was expensive, but I am really glad we did it. It was wonderful to see the girls and their friends all having fun and to meet their school and university friends. It felt like a real landmark moment and it was worth all the effort – it had been a year in the planning – because it was such a success." ANNABEL, MOTHER OF TWO

"The combined 18th and 21st party we had for our son and daughter was lovely, without costing a fortune. We have a typical long, narrow town-house garden, but they wanted the party there, with twinkling lights and so on. Though the garden is pretty small we created several different areas, which I think is quite important, by dividing things up with a gazebo in the middle, a seating area of garden furniture at the back and space to chat on the patio at the front. We made three other seating areas, with chairs and little tables from the house, all of which were colonised by different groups through the evening.

"I was reluctant to shell out too much on hiring a marquee, and anyway had left it a bit late to hire one for a summer weekend that was only three months away when we started organising the party. We solved the problem by investing £150 (a fraction of the cost of hiring even a very small marquee) in a fixed-frame self-assembly gazebo from the DIY store. We slapped some white paint on the nasty brown wood frame, which then looked very good with the cream canvas roof, and I got loads of very cheap white muslin, which we draped to give an exotic Indian tent effect. We added some mirrored baubles and fairy lights and the whole thing looked fantastic, especially when we lit loads of candles and night lights in jars and put them all round the garden. And we still have the gazebo, stored in the shed in bits, in case we ever have another big party.

"We assembled the gazebo the day before, but did not try out the decorations until the day. That is one thing I think was a mistake. It all looked brilliant (just) in time for the party, but we had a few setbacks along the way and tempers got a bit frayed. Another time I would have a proper decoration 'dress rehearsal' at least one day before. Also, we didn't consider flooring until the last minute, and were very lucky that a friend was able to lend us a vast square of old carpet, which virtually covered the lawn, and saved it from complete destruction. Another time I would get that organised well in advance. It was just something I didn't think of.

"The one thing we splashed out on was to have catered canapés at the beginning of the party. That was great. I had made vast quantities of solid food for later (coronation chicken, couscous and salad, with yummy chocolate brownies instead of birthday cake) but having lovely canapés prepared in the kitchen and served for us in the garden took one whole layer of worry away, and I was actually able to enjoy the beginning of the party without having to think about food. For music the birthday boy and girl chose their favourite 18 and 21 tracks respectively, and made an iPod playlist which lasted for the first few hours of the party, with speakers rigged up in the garden." LEANNE, MOTHER OF TWO

"I went to an amazingly smart 21st party in a chateau, where we had to dress up in 19th century costume. It was all quite remarkable, but the thing that stuck in my mind is that when we went to bed, wherever we were staying, all 400 guests had a goody bag on their bed with a personalised mug, some chocolate, some Alka-Seltzer and a little personal note from our host." JONATHAN

## Instead of a big party

Some people really don't want a serious party but still want to celebrate a big birthday with due ceremony. Here are some variously-priced ideas that we know have been successful:

★ Lunch in Paris – if you book far enough ahead the Eurostar tickets are much cheaper and there is certainly no shortage of good restaurants.

★ Learning to drive a tank. Boy heaven (and some girls, too, of course). You can do a full day or a half-day with individual instruction and you even get a choice of which type of tank. Other options include hot air ballooning, hovercrafting or hang gliding.

- A day at Silverstone gives a small group of car-mad individuals the chance to sample one of a thrilling range of driving experiences on the same tarmac as the heroes of motorsport. Drive a Ferrari or a racing car or learn the techniques of rally driving in the home of the British Grand Prix. There is even a Rally Sport Trainer driving session for ten to 17 year olds.
- Hiring a suite at a posh hotel for a sleepover with a difference. Lulu, the lucky girl who inspired this one, celebrated her 18th birthday with a suite for the night at the Georges V in Paris with a couple of girlfriends, waking up to cake and champagne and 18 presents around her bed. It would work pretty well in less exalted surroundings, too.
- Tea at Claridge's/The Ritz/anywhere really posh. Always bliss. Breakfast works just as well.

"Our son wanted something different for his 21st, having been to lots of very enjoyable, but ultimately interchangeable, conventional parties, and we all felt it would be nice to mark the day with something truly memorable. He and his friends are all very keen on fast cars, and we discovered the possibility of a driving 'experience' at Silverstone. Having chosen the option of driving Lotus Elises, we started off with lunch for the ten boys and assorted spectators and then went off to Silverstone. We had one instructor per car, and one car between two boys. They each had one round to get used to the circuit, then three rounds going progressively faster. The instructor was always on board, and reassuringly he had a power button so that he could cut the engine on the car if necessary. This meant that it was all quite safe, but it was very exciting nonetheless. The boys doing the driving had a wonderful time, and it was fun for the spectators, too. The boys were given photos and a DVD and certificate at the end, but it was a memorable day anyway. The instructors were brilliant, and at the end of the day they drove us round the course hair-raisingly fast, which put our efforts into perspective. Then it was back home for the champagne that the drivers had had to do without earlier. It was a great day; by no means cheap, but not in the price bracket of a traditional 21st either." ROGER, FATHER OF THREE

## What makes a party great?

One thing is clear from all the people we've talked to. The parties that people remember the best, and the ones that mean the most to them, whether something simple like playing horses in the garden or a complicated murder mystery where someone has spent ages working out the plot, whether a teddy bears' picnic in the park or a party in a chateau with personal goody bags for 400, are united by the fact that someone has made a real effort and expended lots of thought and ingenuity. It really isn't about the budget, it's all about the care and attention. It's about working out what someone you care about will really enjoy, and making it happen.